Towards reading

RETHINKING READING

Series Editor: L. John Chapman

Current titles:

Eleanor Anderson	*Reading the Changes*
Trevor H. Cairney	*Teaching Reading Comprehension*
Robin Campbell	*Reading Real Books*
Robin Campbell	*Reading Together*
L. John Chapman	*Reading: From 5–11 years*
Christine Davis and Rosemary Stubbs	*Shared Reading in Practice*
Alison Littlefair	*Reading All Types of Writing*
Tony Martin	*The Strugglers: Working with children who fail to learn to read*
Tony Martin and Bob Leather	*Readers and Texts in the Primary Years*
Linda Miller	*Towards Reading: Literacy development in the pre-school years*
Judith Smith and Anne Alcock	*Revisiting Literacy: Helping readers and writers*
Richard Walker *et al.*	*Teaching All the Children to Read*

Towards reading

Literacy development in the pre-school years

LINDA MILLER

Open University Press
Buckingham · Philadelphia

Open University Press
Celtic Court
22 Ballmoor
Buckingham
MK18 1XW

and
1900 Frost Road, Suite 101
Bristol, PA 19007, USA

First Published 1996

A catalogue record of this book is available from the British Library

ISBN 0 335 19216 5 (hb) 0 335 19215 7 (pb)

Library of Congress Cataloging-in-Publication Data

Miller, Linda, 1946–
Towards reading : literacy development in the pre-school years / Linda Miller.
p. cm. — (Rethinking reading)
Includes bibliographical references (p.) and index.
ISBN 0–335–19216–5 (hb). — ISBN 0–335–19215–7 (pb)
1. Reading (Preschool) 2. Language arts (Preschool) 3. Reading––Parent participation. 4. Reading readiness. I. Title. II. Series: Rethinking reading.
LB1140.5.R4L55 1995
372.4—dc20 95–14679
CIP

Typeset by Dorwyn Ltd, Rowlands Castle, Hants
Printed in Great Britain by St Edmundsbury Press Ltd
Bury St Edmunds, Suffolk

For
Chloe and Katie
with love
December 1995

Contents

List of figures

Acknowledgements

My thanks are due to my daughters Chloe and Katie for sowing the seeds for this book and for helping me to see literacy with a new eye. To John Chapman, for giving me the opportunity to write this book and for assuring me that I could do so. To Robin Campbell for unstinting help, support and encouragement and for constructive comments on the manuscript. To Cindy Willey for inviting me to learn about literacy alongside the children, parents and staff in Wall Hall Nursery School, and for her encouraging comments on the manuscript. Finally, to my husband, Peter Miller, for helping to create the time and space for me to write.

Introduction

At the age of 4 years 10 months my elder daughter Chloe started school and began to bring home a 'book bag', i.e. a plastic zip-up folder containing picture and story books which she had chosen. A parent booklet invited comments upon the books shared. This was welcomed as an extension of previous home experiences with books. Enjoyment of the books was emphasized by the teacher rather than 'formal' attempts to teach Chloe to read. Books continued to be shared willingly at home for some time; these included 'home' books, library books and now, books from school. However, towards the end of the first term Chloe ceased to bring home picture and story books and began to bring home 'reading' books, as she had now 'made a start on reading'. There followed a great reluctance on Chloe's behalf to share these books and coercion tactics were needed to persuade her to 'read'. Sharing the books she brought home from school was no longer a pleasure but a chore and many were declared 'boring'. There were exceptions, such as the *Story Chest* (1982) series which seemed to fit some of Waterland's (1985) criteria of a 'worthwhile book'. A family policy evolved of continuing to share the sort of books which had always been enjoyed at home and sharing any school books which Chloe wished to read. However, the continuity between sharing and reading books at home and reading in school seemed to have been broken. In the last year of infant school Chloe, as a fluent reader, was again bringing home books of her own choice.

On reflection there seemed to be an implicit message from the school; that is, both before and after you learn to read you are encouraged to experience a wide range of varied and interesting books, but in between times you learn to read from reading books (Miller, 1990). This is not to deny that for many able and enthusiastic readers, like Chloe, reading scheme books will have been part of their early literacy experiences (Beard, 1987). However, other varied and complex factors will have contributed to this reading development, particularly strong parental interest and a home environment which provides opportunities for literacy (Clark, 1976; Topping, 1985; Wells, 1985; 1987; Tizard *et al.*, 1988).

A further series of personal events stimulated my interest in the role that parents and the home environment play in facilitating the development of early literacy skills, long before formal schooling begins. My awareness grew of these emerging skills in my younger daughter Katie, between the ages of 2½ and 3½ years. A typical event took place in the local Farm Shop where 3½-year-old Katie's attention was caught by a poster advertising bananas:

Katie: What does it say?
Mother: Flavour Value Flavour.

After we returned home, she referred to the carrier bags we had used as 'bags with writing on them'.

A range of observations demonstrated her increasing awareness of print in the environment, a growing interest in writing and books of all kinds, and a developing knowledge about print and books (Clay, 1979; Hall, 1987; Miller, 1991). This wealth of knowledge had developed without any formal teaching, although it has to be acknowledged that Katie's home environment probably fits Heath's (1982) description of a 'mainstream family'; that is representing 'mainstream, middle class, school oriented culture' (p. 49). It seemed, therefore, that the period before formal schooling begins provides fertile ground in which to cultivate and support young children's developing interest in literacy.

Recent research points to literacy development as a continuum which begins with events in the home. For example, the baby playing with soft alphabet blocks or parent and child sharing a book together. This view of literacy development suggests that it is difficult to pinpoint a time when literacy learning begins; learning about literacy is now seen as a continuous process which has its roots in the everyday activities of the home (Teale and Sulzby, 1986). What is certain is, that for the majority of children, reading and writing do not have their starting point in formal educational settings.

This book is written both for, and about, the many people who may be involved in the life of the pre-school child – parents or other primary carers, grandparents, brothers and sisters, and all those working in a professional capacity with young children. To describe the latter, I have mainly used Nutbrown's term 'professional educator' which means 'adults who have some relevant training and qualifications and understand something of how children learn, and who are active in their thinking and interaction with children in group settings' (Nutbrown, 1994, p. x). However, the term 'early years educator' is also used interchangeably. These might include teachers involved in pre-school and early years education and other adults working with young children in a variety of pre-school settings. To describe this range of settings I have employed the description 'centre-based learning' from the *Start Right* report (Ball, 1994). This includes nursery and reception classes in primary schools, day nurseries, combined nursery centres, childcare centres, family centres and playgroups (Ball, 1994).

This book starts from the premise that most of the adults described are already involved in supporting young children in their literacy development, albeit in different ways. One purpose of this book is to highlight the importance of these various adults and different settings, in providing for and supporting literacy development in the pre-school years. A key aim is to raise awareness about the importance of literacy in the lives of young children. Also, to consider what literacy development looks like in the earliest years (Goodman, 1984). The ways in which parents are already supporting and nurturing their children's literacy development, albeit in different contexts and in different ways, are described. It is proposed that parents and professional educators can work together to share what they know about the child's developing knowledge of literacy. A range of projects which have attempted to do this are reported and a framework for implementing such a project is suggested.

Later chapters consider how literacy development can be observed and recorded. A case is made for the provision for literacy in a range of pre-school settings, which parallel literacy experiences in the home. However, it is contended that provision for literacy is not enough, and so the crucial role of the adult in young children's literacy development is defined. A final plea is made for parents and professional educators to work in partnership, in order to reduce the distance between home and pre-school (Gregory and Biarnès, 1994), so that pre-school centres can either provide or supplement what the child has not yet experienced, or as is more likely, can build upon the rich foundations of literacy in the home.

CHAPTER 1

The emergence of literacy

Katie aged 3 years 4 months was sitting on the toilet, she pointed to the 'Shires' name plate on the toilet cistern and asked, 'What does it say?', I replied 'Shires'. Such an incident is probably typical of many which take place throughout a day shared with a young child, but a closer look tells us something about what Katie knows about reading and writing. She knows that the pattern of the silver capital letters on the plastic name plate are different from other patterns, i.e. they 'say' something (contain information), and that the written symbols represent speech. She knows something about the act of reading, that what is written down can be read. She also knows that print is not just found in books (similar incidents relate to writing on carrier bags and posters). She believes that I can read and she can't, and she has a view of the adult as someone who will read for her. So, this one incident, lasting for just a few seconds, is a 'language story' from which we can derive 'literacy lessons' (Harste *et al.*, 1984). It tells us quite a lot about the development which has taken place whilst Katie has been at home with her parents and childminder; that is, before the beginning of any sort of pre-school education in a group setting.

Much of what is written in this and subsequent chapters, will come as no surprise to parents and others who share their personal or professional lives with young children. However, it seems important that what parents and other significant adults may be doing implicitly to support and extend their children's literacy development in the pre-school years, should be made explicit, in order to identify those experiences which seem to contribute to that development. In this chapter some key ideas about early reading and writing development are explored. Also, some terms which are used to describe that development are explained, so that a common language can be shared.

Readiness for reading

It was once thought that there was a magical moment, somewhere between the ages of 5 and 7 years, when children were ready to read, and that the teaching of reading should not begin before this time; hence the term 'reading readiness' (Adams, 1990). Children's pre-reading skills were matched against checklists and tests which contained items thought to be the necessary skills for making a formal start upon reading. The more detailed of these tests included sections on general intelligence, vision, hearing, the home environment. Tasks more specifically related to reading and writing skills might include matching printed letters and words which are the same, or recognizing that two words begin with the same sound. Children's performance on these tests were thought to give a strong indication of their readiness to begin formal reading instruction (Downing and Thackray, 1972). The assumption underlying reading readiness, therefore, was that children must have certain knowledge, skills and information before other forms could be meaningfully learned (Harste *et al.*, 1984). Linked to this was the notion that children had to wait until they were ready before they could have a reading book (Nutbrown and Hannon, 1993).

Many of the items included in such tests and checklists have been shown to have some association with later reading achievement. An example of this is that children aged between 3 and 5 years, who are aware of rhyme, similar sounding initial letters (alliteration) and the sounds and names of letters which make up words, do seem to make better progress in reading than those who are not (Bryant and Bradley, 1985; Adams, 1990; Goswami and Bryant, 1990). However, what seems likely is, that such skills in young children are an indicator of the sorts of informal learning which have been taking place in the pre-school years (as the example of Katie shows). A helpful way of imagining this development is to think of skills such as knowing the names and sounds of the letters of the alphabet as the 'tip of the iceberg' (see Figure 1.1); these are the very visible signs of literacy development. Below the iceberg are all the incidents and activities in daily life which will have contributed to the development showing at the 'tip'. So, the fact that some young children possess those skills which prepare them well for reading in school, is a consequence of their experiences with literacy in the pre-school years; skills such as pointing out familiar letters in a book are a product of the opportunities the children have had to develop these skills, but in an informal way. These opportunities might include regular book sharing with an adult, playing with alphabet games, reading the food packets in the supermarket. Research suggests that formally teaching specific 'pre-reading' skills in isolation to very young children, does not seem to help later reading achievement (Adams, 1990).

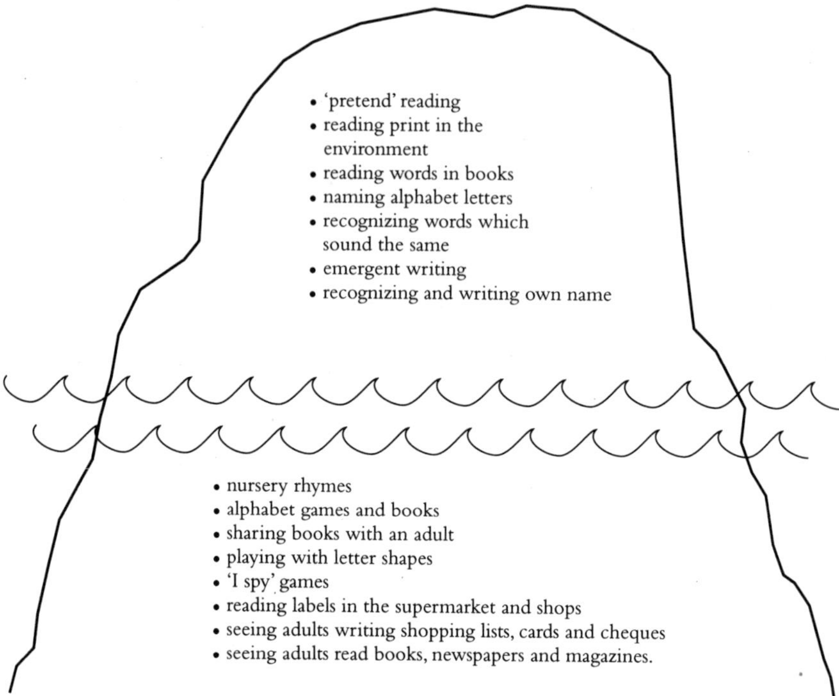

Figure 1.1 The tip of the iceberg

We are also now much more aware that attempting to assess young children's knowledge with tests such as those previously described can be very misleading. The children's responses often depend upon how questions are asked, and also upon how well they have understood what they are being asked to do (Donaldson, 1978). There are more fruitful ways of finding out what young children know about literacy as will be seen in Chapter 8.

There is no doubt that some skills which are learned informally in the pre-school years, do seem to give an advantage to children when they begin to be involved in the more formal teaching of reading. What is questioned, is whether the types of 'reading readiness' activities to be found, for example in some pre-school centres, or in often expensive commercial publications bought by parents, involving activities such as matching and distinguishing pictures, letters and shapes, are either necessary, or indeed helpful to the young child. An alternative view of early reading and writing development can be proposed.

Emergent literacy

The term emergent literacy is currently being used to describe the beginnings of reading and writing development and has replaced notions of 'reading readiness'. It describes what young children come to know about literacy in the pre-school years and how they come to know about it. The term 'emergent literacy' gives rise to ideas about growing and developing, but applied to the areas of reading and writing skills. This view of literacy development suggests something which is in the process of becoming, i.e. there is no one point when children 'read' or 'write'; these skills gradually emerge, and they emerge without formal teaching in the pre-school years (Teale and Sulzby, 1986). Research in the last ten years or so, has shown that for almost all children living in a literate society, learning about literacy begins very early in life. Goodman (1984) uses the very apt phrase 'roots of literacy' to describe the beginnings of reading and writing. To continue the garden theme, her suggestion is that the home environment provides very fertile soil in which the roots of reading and writing can flourish. According to Goodman, literacy roots are nourished in the pre-school years by the type, amount and quality of what she calls 'functional literacy', that is, literacy which is used in real life contexts and serves a real purpose in people's lives. Thus the child might see and be involved with adults writing shopping lists, greetings cards and letters, or reading books, newspapers, the Koran or the Bible. In addition, the attitude of significant adults – parents, grandparents, childminders, towards literacy, also counts, i.e. whether reading and writing is seen to be important in their lives. For example, my own children know the importance of writing for me; at the time of writing, requests for sausages and beans for tea have had to be deferred until the end of a few more paragraphs!

It is, however, quite possible, as Goodman (1984) suggests, and I would add even likely, that busy parents or professional educators may not always be aware of reading and writing development happening. The roots of literacy may be deeply buried in the soil of the busy home environment. Similarities can be seen with the iceberg example in Figure 1.1. Much development goes unnoticed until a root suddenly gives rise to a shoot in the form of the child recognizing a familiar letter or word. Again Katie serves as an example here. The incident on the toilet is one that could have easily been missed by the adult busily cleaning out the bathroom; it is certainly unlikely that the typical parent would analyse the incident in the way that I have done. As it happens, in the incident described, Katie's 'literacy roots' received a little more nurturing; however, I am sure there have been as many missed opportunities. As Leichter (1984) pointed out, much education in the home takes place on a 'moment-to-moment' basis. It arises from everyday events such as a cooking or shopping session, and therefore opportunities are easily missed in the business of family life.

It is therefore suggested that notions of pre-readers and pre-writers, reading readiness and pre-reading skills have no place within this view of emergent literacy, the child is not seen as pre-anything. Early reading and writing development arises out of what is happening in an everyday context, which will, of course, differ within every family depending upon factors such as culture, economics or time available to spend with children. Meek (1991) describes literacy as emerging from the social background of children's lives. So, reading and writing development, rather than beginning at a certain point (i.e. on entry to school), is seen as a continuum of development along which each child moves at an individual pace (Teale and Sulzby, 1986; Strickland and Cullen, in Adams, 1990). Progress along this continuum will depend upon many of the factors previously mentioned.

If key adults in children's lives are unaware of the sorts of literacy development which can take place in the pre-school years, then opportunities for supporting and furthering this development will be missed. Once again Goodman (1984) proves helpful in identifying these emerging skills, which she describes under the headings of the three major roots of literacy:

- *The functions and forms of literacy*
  This includes a growing awareness in the child of the many purposes which literacy can serve and the different forms which it can take. Examples might be showing awareness of print in familiar situations, e.g. a STOP sign when out in the car, or McDonalds when out for a burger treat; or an awareness of connected print found in books, magazines and newspapers. The child may also begin to show a developing knowledge about writing such as the purpose it serves (to write the shopping list) and the use of implements for writing.
- *Using oral language about written language*
  This involves the ability of children to talk about the literacy events in which they are involved, perhaps in a book-sharing situation using words such as book, word, read, write. Katie illustrated this when she asked 'What does that say?'. 'Say' is often used by young children to refer to 'read' when talking about language which is written down (Goodman, 1984).
- *Conscious knowledge about literacy*
  This is when children have developed a conscious knowledge, rather than intuitive awareness, of what reading and writing are about. Reading and writing come to be seen by the child as objects or events which can be talked about. Again Katie springs to mind, when sharing a picture book she said 'That's an "e" like in my name', and when writing 'Is it good to do a dot like that?' when writing an 'i' (Miller, 1991).

No doubt many adults living and working with young children can recall similar examples under these headings. Indeed, jotting down and dating such incidents, and collecting dated samples of children's early attempts at mark making, can be a simple and illuminating way of recording young children's growing knowledge about literacy, as will be seen in Chapter 8.

To summarize the main theme of this chapter: finding out what young children know about literacy has engaged many researchers over the last decade and is explored further in the next two chapters. This research has led to a view of literacy development as a continuum of development which can begin in the first weeks of life, when the child's room is decorated with murals, bedspreads and stuffed animals that represent characters in books (Heath, 1982). Children's progress along this continuum will depend upon the amount of support and encouragement they receive from parents, other significant adults and professional educators in the pre-school years.

CHAPTER 2

Towards reading: what children come to know

Some time ago I was involved in setting up a book-sharing project in a pre-school playgroup, which aimed to encourage parents and their children to share books together on a regular basis (Miller, 1992). In order to find out if the project was having a positive effect, I needed to know what the children's knowledge about books was at the beginning and the end of the project. Discovering what these 31 children knew about books and print before the project began was one of the most exciting and interesting outcomes.

The majority of these 3- and 4-year-olds, who were embarking upon their first experience of pre-school education outside the home setting, already had considerable knowledge about books and stories. They knew how to handle a book, i.e. which way up to hold it; they could show the front and the back of the book and could turn the pages in a front to back direction. All but 3 of the children knew which were the pictures and 22 children could point to the writing when asked. When asked what a letter was, 17 children knew and when asked to point to a letter which was the same as the one selected by the adult, 21 children could do this. The first letter of a word was known by 6 children and 3 could show the last letter, thus showing that they were beginning to recognize individual letters as part of whole words. The knowledge that a left page should be read before a right was demonstrated by 18 of the children and 4 knew the direction in which the print should be read. Many of the children also knew about the sort of language which is used to tell stories, as they were able to tell a familiar story back to an adult; an activity many adults will recognize as 'pretend' reading.

It needs to be emphasized that these children were fairly typical of the range of children who might be found in the playgroup of a large village. Their parents' occupations ranged from an ambulance driver to university teacher, although more were engaged in 'professional' jobs than might be expected for the general population and none was unemployed. What these children knew about written language and books had been learned from their experiences at home with their parents and other significant adults.

This project is reported here in some detail, because it raises a number of questions. A key question is how this group of children came to know so much about at least one aspect of early literacy development, i.e. knowledge about books, before any teaching in a formal setting had taken place. Arising from this, the question has to be asked, why many children on beginning pre-school or primary school are treated as if they do not know anything about literacy? (Harste *et al.*, 1984; Hall, 1985; Baker and Raban, 1991). These are questions which I will return to in subsequent chapters. They are raised here as a focus for the reader, as Chapters 2 and 3 attempt to summarize the extent of knowledge about written language which children bring not only to primary school at age 4 or 5 years, but to the pre-school at a considerably earlier age.

Towards reading

It seems inappropriate to separate reading and writing in a book about early literacy development, especially as the 'wholeness' of that development is emphasized (Holdaway, 1979). The fact that the emergence of reading and writing are closely linked is frequently stressed (Hall, 1987; Campbell, 1992). However, in order to increase awareness and understanding of the way in which these two key skills develop, it can be useful to take a close look at each, whilst at the same time understanding that they are inextricably linked. Ferreiro (1984) acknowledged this dilemma, stating 'Developmental literacy cannot be understood by isolating some of its components from others', but goes on to say 'it seems very hard to analyze all the components at the same time and in the same depth' (p. 154). Therefore a separate look will be taken at these two aspects of early literacy development.

Print in the environment

Recognizing print in the environment can be one of the first signs of emerging literacy skills in young children, as Meek (1982, p. 41) has written:

> Hundreds of children have learned to read from advertisements on hoardings . . . They guess the meaning of what they see; the surrounding context provides the feedback of whether they are right or wrong, and gradually as they did in play, they look for individual words and letters.

I recently observed a little boy and his mother making their way through the car park outside the local playgroup; as they passed a line of parked cars the child's attention seemed to be caught by a number plate on one of the cars. Both mother and child spent some time crouching down to look carefully at, point to and talk about the letters and numbers. As they were out of earshot, it was only possible to speculate that the child's attention had been caught by a letter or number that had some special significance for him.

Opportunities such as this present themselves in numerous everyday situations; for example, shopping in the supermarket and noticing familiar labels on food packets, or repeatedly seeing the EXIT sign on leaving the car park. The significance of the print will in many cases be linked to the social experience or event to which it relates. 'Coco Pops' is not just a label on a cereal packet, for many children the familiar packet on the breakfast table is part of a daily social experience linked to the routine of breakfast. It is also a sugary, milky, chocolatey, pleasurable sensory experience, all of which gives added significance to the print. Finding and recognizing the label on the supermarket shelf then has a real function – if the right packet isn't found then breakfasts may be less pleasurable in the following week. Thus, this type of reading 'game' becomes a significant and important part of early literacy development.

Taylor (1983) in her study of six families in their home setting, documented the ways in which learning to 'read' signs and print in the environment was deeply embedded in the daily lives of the children, and almost always had a function, e.g. pointing out the WAIT sign on the pedestrian crossing. Harste *et al.* (1984) cite a similar incident with Alison, aged 4, who, after depositing the remains of her ice-cream cone through the PUSH flap of the rubbish bin, 'read' the word PUSH. They make the point that it is from knowing what written language does that children become aware of the form it takes, and are subsequently able to 'read' it. Yet, as Taylor noted, such opportunities are easily missed and the child's comments or actions can pass unnoticed (see also Leichter, 1984). No doubt on a busier morning the little boy in the car park may have been rushed off to the shops or to the playgroup.

A number of researchers have attempted to capture such incidents by documenting their own children's growing recognition of print in the environment (Lass, 1983; Payton, 1984; Miller, 1990; 1991; Laminack, 1991). Collected observations of my younger daughter Katie illustrate a typical incident. At age 3 years 5 months she presented me with the card game 'Whot' which she had not played before, she pointed to the letters on the pack and declared 'This says "Snap"'. She then proceeded to 'read' the instructions for the game with comments such as 'and then you put the cards there' in language quite different to the 'story' language used when pretend reading her books. Although Katie's guess (or hypothesis) about the name of the game was incorrect, nevertheless she had formulated a reasonable alternative on the basis of her previous experience with print in a similar context. She also demonstrated an expectation that the written print associated with the game would have meaning and a language relevant to the game. Harste *et al.* (1984) argued that such continuing encounters with print allow children to test out the viability of the guesses they make about print in the environment. It is by putting repeated guesses or hypotheses to the test, that children come to have a meaning base for making sense of the written language around them. Laminack (1991) suggests that this is the way in which children move from gross approximations about print to conventional reading.

Some researchers have opted for a more experimental approach in attempting to establish whether young children read print in the environment. In a study of 3- and 4-year-olds Hiebert (1978) found that when presented with 10 examples of environmental print, both with and without environmental clues, that is, clues from the situation in which the print is found, the children used environmental cues and were not just reading the print. Also age seemed to play a part as the younger children made more 'errors' (see also Goodall, 1984). A similar study was carried out by Masonheimer *et al.* (1984) with 102, 3–5 year-olds, but they altered the letters within familiar logos. The results showed that only 6 children identified as 'readers' noted the changes. Masonheimer *et al.* claimed the remainder were 'reading' the environmental cues and not the print (see also Goswami, 1994).

It has already been argued that studies which place young children in strange environments and present them with tasks taken out of a real life context, may not be the best way to find out what young children know. Hall (1987) made this point when describing Kastler's (1984) research with 5- and 6-year-old children, which used more child-sensitive methods. The children were questioned about 21 items of print on familiar objects such as catalogues, newspapers, library cards, advertisements. Only the library card did not give rise to an appropriate response.

In 'reading' environmental print, the young child may not look beyond the background information to concentrate on the print, as might happen, for example, in a book-sharing situation when the adult points to the words being read. Adults would therefore seem to play a crucial role; as Laminack (1991, p. 88) says:

> Unless adults draw attention to print and help children associate it with their own words, ideas and experiences, youngsters may not make strong connections between print and their own lives. It is through interactions with other people that children begin to understand the various functions print can serve in their culture.

Taylor (1983) observed 'plenty of evidence' of children in the families she studied recognizing print in the environment, but says, 'We can only guess what it is the child reads' (p. 63). It would seem, therefore, that environmental print does have a role to play in leading children along the path towards reading. Young children from a range of cultures have opportunities for noticing print in the environment as part of a wide range of early literacy experiences. In their work with Bengali families in London, Gregory and Rashid (1992–3) describe the range of print and print-related materials in the home language to be found amongst the shops providing items for everyday living in the Brick Lane area, e.g. books, magazines, posters and videos. It is possible to speculate that one important function of environmental print is that it enables the child to behave like a reader, allowing parents and others to praise the child's efforts. This may help to build a positive attitude towards reading. In other words, an important function of environmental print could be the use to which it is put by significant adults in the pre-school years. It would therefore seem important that adults working professionally with young children, ensure that encounters with environmental print are part of the young child's everyday experience.

Concepts about print

Finding out what young children know about written language is a task which has engaged a number of researchers in the last decade. The findings from a group of studies which investigated pre-schoolers' knowledge about an area of written language known as 'concepts about print' were summarized by Lomax and McGee (1987). They showed that pre-school children were:

- learning about the features of letters, i.e. they were beginning to distinguish one letter from another
- could name some letters
- could discriminate between letters, words and sounds
- could read words in familiar settings in the environment, e.g. STOP.

They also documented how some young children were beginning to develop strategies for matching written language on the page to spoken language and were beginning to match letter names with their sounds.

Other research has described young children's ability to handle books appropriately, their knowledge of the direction in which the print should be read and a knowledge of the difference between the words and pictures, i.e. that writing is what you read (Clay, 1977; Lomax and McGee, 1987; Miller, 1992).

Stages of reading development

It has been suggested that early reading development may emerge in a particular sequence. A study of 38 4-year-olds, over a school year led the researcher involved to suggest the following sequence of development relating to word reading:

- *Level 1* – knowledge of the function of print (the ability to read signs and labels)
- *Level 2* – knowledge of the form of print (the ability to learn letter names)
- *Level 3* – knowledge of the conventions of print (the ability to associate letters with sounds) (Mason, 1980; Mason, 1981; 1985, cited in Kontos, 1986).

Building upon this work Lomax and McGee (1987) found that children aged 3 to 6 years expanded their awareness and understanding of different aspects of literacy development with age, i.e.:

- ideas about print (e.g. the direction in which it is read)
- awareness of writing
- awareness of sounds (which make up words)
- letter/sound association
- word reading.

However, the researchers are careful to say that the children did not need to master one of the above areas before going on to the next. For example, some 5- and 6-year-olds were able to read some words, yet were still developing ideas about print and writing.

Sequences of development through which children generally proceed can provide a broad framework within which to observe children. However, if rigidly applied to individuals, there is a danger of 'waiting' for one step of development to occur, before providing the child with experiences and opportunities perceived as relevant for the next stage. To illustrate this point further, in considering the term 'pre-reading level', a phrase sometimes used by primary school teachers to characterize certain children as being 'ready' for a 'reading' book or not, Smith (1986) argued that allocating children to levels in this way, may cut them off from certain valuable experiences and opportunities. Harste *et al.* (1984) also warn against the use of 'developmental yardsticks' to measure the process of literacy development. In other words, looking for specific indicators of development such as letter or word recognition, can divert attention away from other important aspects of children's learning about written language. Learning about literacy will differ from child to child and will be affected by the sorts of literacy experiences they encounter (Teale and Sulzby, 1986).

Phonological awareness

Phonological awareness involves the knowledge that words that are spoken can be broken down into component parts (Meek, 1993). It involves the ability to detect sounds within words, for example knowing whether sounds like 'pin' and 'win' rhyme with each other, or whether words like 'sock' and 'sun' begin with the same sound (alliteration). Also important is the ability to tap out the number of sounds in a spoken word, e.g. 'c-a-t' and detecting how sounds are broken up into smaller units, e.g. 'spr/ing', i.e. the onset and rime (Goswami, 1994). Awareness of rhyme appears to develop before children can read conventionally. Chukovsky (1971) collected observations of young children's language which showed their fascination with rhymes and rhyming words. Three-year-old Bubus demonstrates this:

> Grandma thinks I'm dandy
> She always brings me candy.
>
> (p. 68)

It has been found that young children who are aware of rhyme and alliteration, subsequently tend to be successful at reading. In the previous chapter it was suggested that experiences in the home play a large part in the development of this knowledge. For example, involvement in hearing nursery rhymes, songs, jingles and tongue twisters and playing 'I spy' games (Bryant and Bradley, 1985; Goswami, 1994). Goswami (1994) says, 'It is now well established that there is a strong connection between children's ability to detect and manipulate the sounds making up spoken words and their reading development'. She goes on to cite Bryant and Bradley, 'phonological ability in pre-school children is one of the biggest predictors of later success in reading ability' (p. 32).

Children's awareness of reading

Young children appear to have an awareness of what people do when they read and write; however, tapping this knowledge can tax the ingenuity of the most experienced and sensitive of researchers as Hall (1988) demonstrated. He wanted to find out what nursery age children knew about both reading and writing, but did so by asking them if animals could learn to read and write (which most found very amusing). Nearly all were sure that animals could not do so because they did not have hands to hold the pen or the book; to quote one child 'They ain't got no hands.' Another equally sensible suggestion was 'They can't talk' (p. 150). Hall concluded that reading and writing were seen by these children as a very physical and essentially human activity, i.e. 'reading is holding something printed and saying the words', and 'writing is apparently exclusively the ability physically to grasp a pen or pencil and make certain kinds of movements'

(p. 154). He suggested that these explanations should not be surprising as they link with children's experience of, for example, being read to aloud.

In the first instance this seems to make sense, as children's main experience of reading is of having a book read aloud to them. However, an alternative interpretation is possible. It may be that the children were just trying to work out why animals cannot read and write. I include this example to illustrate the difficulties of finding the right questions to 'test' young children's knowledge, even when the researcher is as skilled and sensitive as Nigel Hall. Hall also described an incident in which his niece, when asked what her mother was doing replied 'Nothing, she's just looking at the paper'; thus, he argued, silent reading was not viewed as a type of reading by his niece (Hall, 1988, p. 154). However, two similar, but contradictory, incidents from my own experience spring to mind. In a rare moment of enjoying reading the paper in the sunshine in the garden, I was asked by my then 3-year-old daughter, 'What are you doing?', to which I replied 'Reading'; 'You can't be reading because you're talking', was her response. This seemed to imply that she had an idea that silent reading involved a degree of thinking and concentrating, which meant that you could not talk at the same time. The second incident occurred when Katie was aged 4, as I was reading the Sunday newspapers whilst wearing my spectacles. Katie went off and returned with a pair of sunglasses and proceeded to 'read' silently the leaflets from the colour magazine, declaring that she needed her glasses to read. In the study by Baker and Raban (1991), Lucy, by 5 years of age, correctly distinguished between silent reading, reading out loud and 'looking at'. As another example, Laminack (1991), whilst reading his students' exam papers, was asked by his 3½-year-old son Zachary what he was doing, he explained that he was reading. Zachary informed him 'You're supposed to do it this way', moving his lips and barely whispering the words, 'You don't supposed to be quiet when you read' (p. 46).

Like many other children, Katie, Lucy and Zachary will have had considerable exposure to models of reading in the home which will have enabled them to build up an extensive range of ideas about reading, including the fact that it can take a variety of forms. There is no doubt that very young children know more about written language and the activity of reading than can be easily elicited by testing, questioning or trying to observe them in everyday settings. Enabling children to demonstrate what they know about literacy through actively involving them in the process is considered in Chapter 8.

It was stated at the beginning of this chapter that reading and writing development are inextricably linked, yet in order to consider what young children come to know about literacy, this chapter has separated reading from writing. The next chapter therefore moves on to consider what young children come to know about writing.

CHAPTER 3

Towards writing: what children come to know

The point was made in Chapter 1, that parents and professional educators need to be aware of, and alerted to, signs of developing literacy skills in order to support and extend literacy development. It is possible that early writing efforts may be missed or dismissed as unworthy of attention (Harste *et al.*, 1984). Taylor (1983), who studied the reading and writing activities of six families with young children over a three-year period in their own homes, found that many of the children's writing activities were so fleeting that they were often missed by the adult. It was not until I began to collect examples of my younger daughter Katie's early writing attempts, that I realized the range and volume of her productions. These included letters, notices, stories, filled in forms and crosswords, shopping lists, party invitations and home-made books; items which otherwise would no doubt have been consigned unnoticed to the waste bin. Collecting and dating examples of children's emerging writing skills in this way, can provide valuable evidence of a child's ongoing literacy development and is considered further in Chapter 8.

Emergent writing

Emergent writing is defined by Sulzby (1990) as 'the reading and writing behaviours of young children before they develop into conventional literacy' (p. 85). Although the onset of conventional writing is gradual, Sulzby offers a helpful definition:

- writing that another conventional literate person can read conventionally, and
- writing that the child himself or herself reads conventionally.

She goes on to list the many different forms that early writing can take before it becomes conventional, e.g. scribble, drawing, non-phonetic letter strings, copying of conventional print, invented spelling, rebus, abbreviations, pseudoletters and idio-syncratic forms. Such a framework, describing the forms which emergent writing can take, can be of help in locating where children are in their continuum of development.

Forms of writing

Scribble

Young children use a variety of forms of writing which parents and early years educators will recognize. The earliest of these is often described as 'scribble'. When opportunities and materials are made available, children begin repetitive mark making as early as 12–18 months; when the child can grasp an implement such as a crayon and make to and fro lines (Sheridan, 1975). This undifferentiated scribble is the first form of writing to appear in the home setting (Sulzby *et al.*, 1989). Scribble then begins to develop into scribble for writing and scribble for drawing, although as Sulzby (1990) says, the child does not make this clear distinction between drawing and writing until the end of the second or during the third year.

The use of the term 'scribble' is viewed by some researchers (Harste *et al.*, 1984), as an insufficient description of these early writing attempts. They found that by 3 years of age the children they studied were able, under certain conditions, to distinguish between scribble for writing and scribble for drawing. For example, some children would use up/down strokes for 'writing' and circular marks for 'drawing'; however, another child might use the reverse, but one or the other would be used consistently. Interestingly, children whose name began with a linear letter, i.e. 'L', tended to use linear marks for 'writing', whereas if their name began with a curved letter, e.g. 'S', then circular patterns would tend to be used.

A key point made by Harste *et al.* is that scribble is not random mark making, but is organized according to these principles. It was also found that the 3-year-olds in their study moved freely between drawing and writing. What they couldn't write, they drew; thus drawing was used as an important 'keep going strategy' to convey what they wanted to 'say'. What the adult might dismiss as scribble, was found to 'place hold meaning' in the same way as conventional writing does for the skilled writer. They therefore argue that, in scribble, the beginning of the formal written sign can be traced, and that before children have determined what a particular written mark may signify, they have a basic understanding that written marks have 'sign potential', i.e. that they can be used to communicate meaning.

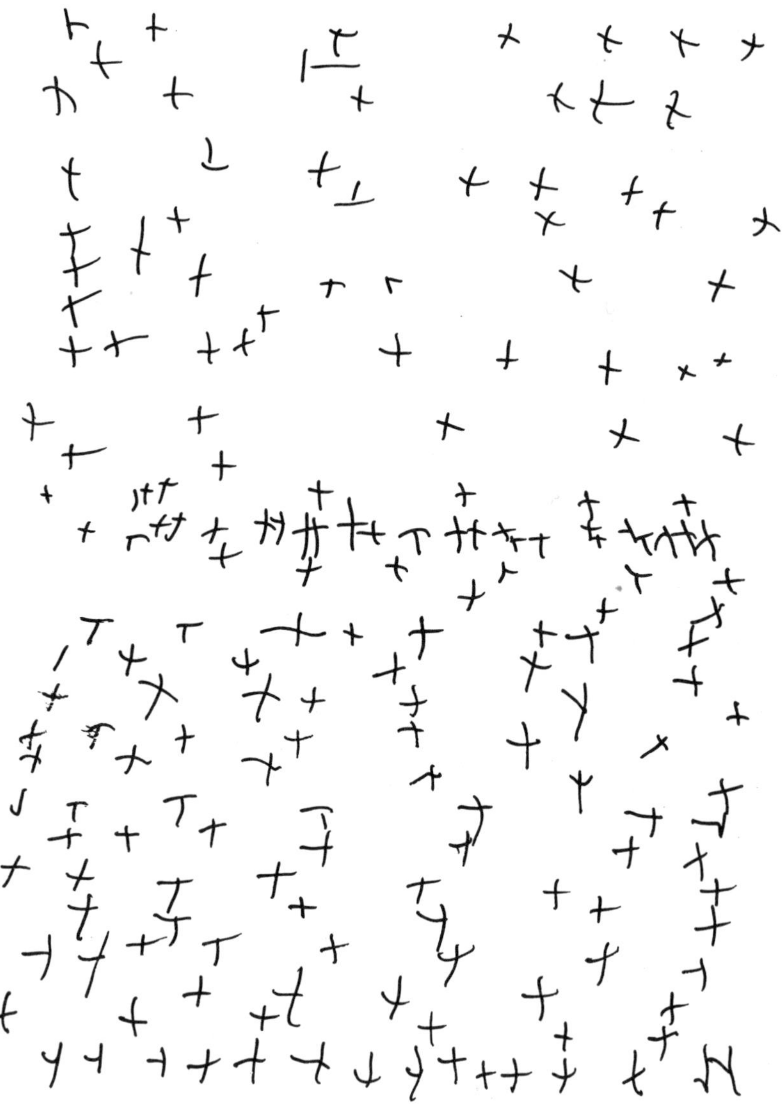

Figure 3.1 A story – 'this is writing?' (Katie aged 3 years 4 months)

Figure 3.2 'Does that say my name?' (Katie aged 3 years 11 months)

These insights into the mark making and writing achievements of very young children proved illuminating in looking through the material collected from my daughter Katie. When aged 3 years 4 months, she sat down alongside her older sister who was writing and produced pages of cross-like marks as shown in Figure 3.1, and asked for confirmation that 'this is writing?'. The piece was then read to her grandmother as a story about a princess, a little girl and a daddy. A later example in Figure 3.2, shows that her written attempts just before her fourth birthday are more 'letter like', however, she still asked 'Does that say my name?' Borrowing from Harste *et al.*'s (1984, p. 108) insights; whilst Katie lacked the knowledge and skills to produce specific marks to make specific meanings, she did understand that the marks she made were 'objects which signify', i.e. represent meaning. Harste *et al.* are convinced that all the children in their study wrote with 'intent to mean' and that it is therefore important to regard scribble not as pre-literate signs, but as the stuff of true literacy.

Writing with letters

Writing with letters covers a large number of writing forms: imitating conventional words, using non-phonetic letter strings, invented spelling and conventional writing (Sulzby, 1990). Around 3 years of age letter-like

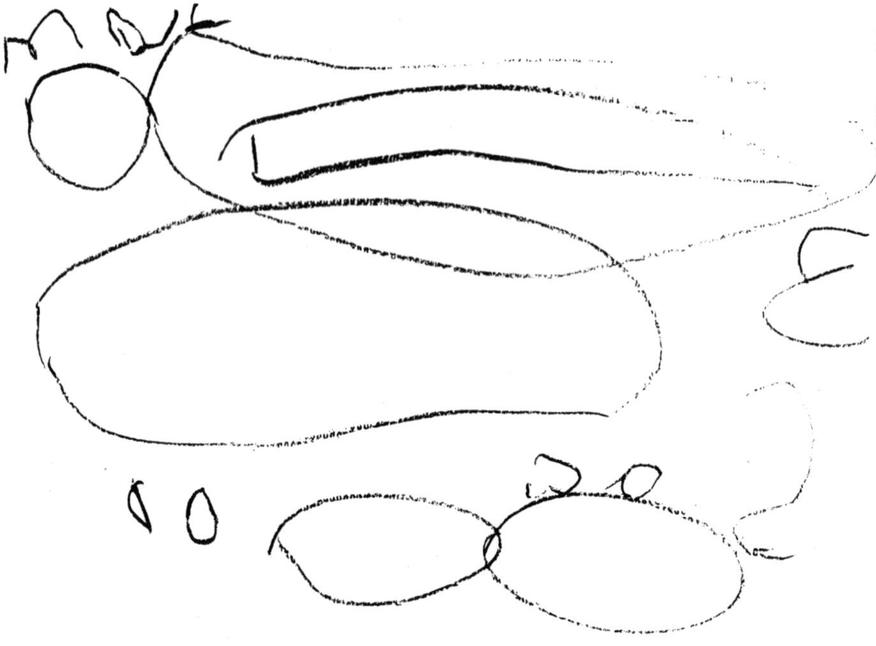

Figure 3.3 *Max's name (Max aged 3 years 6 months)*

features begin to appear in children's writing and drawing as seen in Figure 3.2, including some conventional letters; these reflect the patterns of their culture. Some interesting examples are described by Harste *et al.* (1984). Four-year-old Najeeba from Saudi Arabia had written a very intricate script with lots of 'dots'; she told the researchers 'Here, but you can't read it, cause I wrote it in Arabic and in Arabic we use a lot more dots than you do in English' (p. 82). Cross-cultural concerns, which will be familiar to many anxious parents, were also shared in the research project. The grandmother of Ofer, from Israel, was concerned that his Hebrew-like script was sometimes written 'backwards', left to right being backwards in Hebrew, as opposed to right to left in English. As the researchers point out, these examples support the view that young children are attending to and using the written language they see around them, well before formal schooling begins.

Learning letter names and forms takes place across a long period of development, with letter forms looking 'amazingly common across children', e.g. multi-legged 'E's and reversed letters (Sulzby, 1990, p. 89). Children may also produce familiar words such as 'mummy' or their own name (Davies, 1988; Sulzby *et al.*, 1989). The child's name is often the first stable string of letters produced by the child. Figure 3.3 shows how

3½-year-old Max used his name to mark his drawings done in his day nursery. One task used in Harste *et al.*'s (1984) study was to ask the children to write their name and 'anything else they could write'. They found that all 3-year-olds had developed a marking system which to them represented their own name. An example given is 3-year-old Terry who used the letter 'e' from his name to consistently sign his name. Again to draw upon Katie as an example, certain letters, i.e. 't' and 'k' were consistently used as seen in Figure 3.2, along with a more random selection, to represent her name. Well after the emergence of conventional letters, Sulzby *et al.* (1989) reported that some children produce pseudo 'fast writing', which is no doubt influenced by the adult as a writing model.

Non-phonetic letter strings

Children begin to compose stories or messages using strings of letters that have no phonetic relationship with what they are meant to say, these are called non-phonetic letter strings. Sulzby (1990) divides these into random letter strings, patterned letter strings (e.g. recurring patterns of vowels and consonants) and 'name' elements in which the letters of a name are combined in numerous ways. Children of 3 and 4 years often use a mix of scribble, drawing and strings of letters as Katie's drawing of an elephant shows in Figure 3.4.

Invented spelling

From children's letter strings emerge early attempts at invented spellings. Bissex (1980), in an account of her son Paul's reading and writing development, gives the much quoted example of his invented spelling message to her at the age of 5 years. Having failed to gain her attention by other means when she was engrossed in a book, he stamped out with rubber letter stamps 'rudf' (Are you deaf?). My own daughters discovered the power of 'kpowt' (keep out) notices on their respective bedroom doors, long before they could spell the words conventionally.

Invented spellings appear throughout the ages of 3 to 7 years and have been categorized in a number of ways. Gentry (1982) has used the study of Bissex's son Paul, to describe five stages of development in children's early spelling attempts. These are outlined below:

- *Pre-communicative:* where the child knows that symbols create a message and have a meaning, but may use invented symbols.

Figure 3.4 An elephant (Katie aged 3 years 9 months)

- *Semi-phonetic:* when the child begins to understand that letters 'have' sounds, as in the example 'rudf'. Also, words may be abbreviated and combined with pictures.
- *Phonetic:* when sound and symbol correspondence are used in writing. However, the child may not be aware of the accepted letter strings in English.

Paul's entry into the *Transitional Stage* was not identified by Gentry until Paul entered his sixth year, when he began to use the basic conventions of the English writing system. By the time he was 8 years old Paul had entered Gentry's *Correct Stage.*

Gentry suggests that such 'stages' may be useful to teachers in assessing children's development and in planning strategies for supporting their early writing. However, as is noted in the previous chapter and in Chapter 8, such frameworks need to be cautiously interpreted. Sulzby (1990) has written, 'I do not think, however, that writing can be described as invariant, hierarchically ordered stages' (p. 85). Rather, she suggests, changes in children's writing come about as a result of their new understandings about the system.

Two key categories described by Sulzby (1990) are *syllabic invented spellings,* in which the child uses one letter per syllable and *full invented*

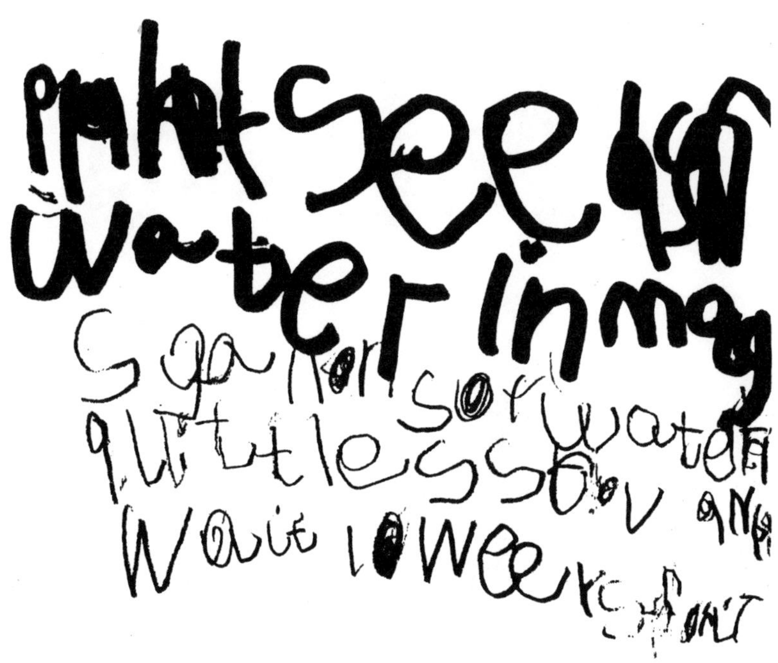

Figure 3.5 Andrew's seed packet

spelling in which one letter per phoneme is used. Sulzby uses the term *intermediate invented spelling* to cover all the development in between.

Three key strategies which children use in moving towards conventional spelling are suggested by Harste *et al.* (1984):

- *Spelling the way it sounds,* i.e. 'jress', 6-year-old Jeff's attempt at 'dress'.
- *Spelling the way it looks,* i.e. 'fro', 5-year-old Sara's attempt at 'for'.
- *Spelling the way it means,* i.e. Sarah's 'wasapanataem' (Once upon a time) which for her signals a whole unit to do with fairy tales (pp. 96–7).

Examples such as these must not be treated as 'wrong' but as a window through which to understand the child's view of how the conventions of written language work. Figures 3.5 and 3.6 show how two reception class children have used invented spelling in designing seed packets for their classroom garden centre. A number of conventionally spelt words such as 'water' and 'seed' can be seen in Andrew's written instructions. Figure 3.6 shows a very good attempt at the word 'tomatoes'. It is through such 'errors' that children demonstrate their current level of understanding and show how they are actively constructing knowledge of how the writing and spelling system works.

Figure 3.6 Tomatoes

Conventional writing

In their third or fourth year children begin to produce some conventionally spelt words. Understanding of this system appears after invented spellings and this development continues well into the primary school years. Spelling the way it sounds, as in phonetic spelling, is not enough in English and children have to begin to use other strategies, such as remembering what words look like (Sulzby, 1990).

Imitating conventional words

This form of writing is mentioned by Sulzby in the context of certain environments for writing, in which the children's task is to copy correct forms. As a total approach it can mask children's knowledge of the writing system. However, having a model of conventional writing in the environment, perhaps in the form of key words linked to topics, can provide a useful resource to support children's writing (Geekie and Raban, 1993).

Less common forms of emergent writing

Some less common forms of emergent writing are described by Sulzby (1990). *Pseudoletters* are 'letter-like scribble', although they may appear after children know a number of conventional letters. *Rebus* (e.g. an eye depicting the long sound 'I') involves an understanding of the sound-symbol relationship and is used quite late in development. It is a strategy which I have seen utilized in reception classes to encourage children to write. They are given a story sheet with key words missing and are asked to insert a rebus or a word to complete the story.

Stages of emergent writing?

The pitfalls associated with segmenting children's development into rigid stages were pointed out in the previous chapter. However, as Sulzby (1990) says, a particular ordering of forms of writing might be useful in assessing children's development, providing the adult is aware that the transition from emergent to conventional writing is both continuous and discontinuous; that is, that writing forms appear and disappear in the course of development. Also, that young children are active problem solvers and constructers of knowledge and will choose from a range of strategies in their attempts to make meaning. These strategies will be dependent upon their literacy learning and experience to date (Hall, 1991). Young children will happily mix letter strings, scribble, drawing, and conventional spelling.

Five stages or levels through which children pass in their development are proposed by Ferreiro (1984) arising from research with young children from a range of social and cultural backgrounds. It was found that initially drawings and graphemes (single written characters) were treated quite separately by the children. At this stage letters did not 'stand for something else'; for example, when asked 'What does this say?' (about their picture), the children replied 'letters'. In other words, letters were seen as objects in their own right. The children also expected the written letter strings to be proportional to age and size. For example, expecting a name to be longer because an object or person is bigger.

As the children began to distinguish between drawing and writing, their attempts at letters were distributed anywhere on the page, rather than in line. Also they were quite likely to be incorporated into the children's drawings (see Figure 3.4).

There was a transitional stage in the children's development when letters only 'say' something because they are near to the picture. For example, letters that say 'cat' in one place, if transferred somewhere else, may say something quite different; their meaning is not yet stable.

An important milestone is when eventually a written sign (or signs) is used for each object or picture/pictures. An example given is three letters for a drawing of three cats. Another claim of Ferreiro's was that the children required there to be a minimum number of three graphemes (plus or minus one) before a piece of writing was viewed as readable.

Figure 3.7 The recurring principle (Katie aged 3 years 8 months)

Clay (1975) provides another way of considering children's writing. She identified what she described as key principles which children aged 4 years 10 months to 7 years used as they emerged as writers. However, no claims for stages of development were made. The principles were:

The recurring principle

This can be seen in children's writing and drawing where the same basic form is repeated, e.g. a repeated drawing of a person or writing of a symbol. This was demonstrated as early as age 3 years 8 months by Katie as shown in Figure 3.7. The use of this principle allows for long messages or stories to be written by using repeated letter strings.

The directional principle

Clay claims that until the directional principle is understood, young children will put letters and signs anywhere on the page. This can be seen in Figure 3.4, where Katie has fitted her name around the drawing. Clay describes four steps that the child needs to master:

1. Start top left.
2. Move left to right across the word or line.
3. Return down left.
4. Locate next starting point.

Katie's letter written almost one month later provides an example in Figure 3.8.

The flexibility principle

Young children are not constrained like adults by the conventions of print, as Ofer's grandmother was seen to note earlier in this chapter. Much to the concern of adults, they reverse letters and lines of writing. Clay suggests this may be due to failure to remember a known pattern, but may also be attributed to children's creativity and a desire to experiment with known patterns. Figure 3.8 shows a number of reversed letter-like signs.

The generating principle

This is when a limited number of known signs are used to produce long statements. A return to Katie's letter illustrates this principle.

Figure 3.8 The directional principle (Katie aged 3 years 9 months)

The inventory principle

This involves children taking stock of their own learning, for example writing lists of all the words they know.

The contrastive principle

Clay illustrates this principle of children contrasting shapes, letters and word meanings by examples such as 'is' 'si' or drawing of a happy or sad face accompanied by the appropriate word.

The abbreviation principle

This occurred more rarely in the 5-year-olds studied, where they intentionally abbreviated a word.

In a discussion of these principles Hall (1987) suggests they 'seem to be simply descriptions of some of the things emergent writers do' (p. 50).

Towards writing

The use of frameworks or sequences of development to aid our understanding of how children learn about literacy is re-visited in Chapter 8, where it is suggested that these may be just one way in which we can come to a better understanding of what young children know and can do. As Sulzby (1986) has written 'I have become convinced that there is not just one developmental sequence that can be found in children's use of writing systems' (p. 70).

What is clear, is that parents, other significant adults and professional educators must let children write in order to allow them to try out their hypotheses or 'best guesses' so that they might discover how the conventional system works and demonstrate what they know. Emergent writing provides illuminating insights into the ways in which even very young children are trying to understand the system. The provision of contexts within which this can happen is the task of the parent and professional educator. The role of the parents in literacy development is the focus of the next chapter.

CHAPTER 4

The role of parents in literacy development

In Chapter 1 the important role of significant adults in supporting and extending young children's literacy development was stressed; for children in the pre-school years this key adult will be the parent or other main caregiver. Tizard and Hughes (1984), citing Bruner quote, 'One of the most crucial ways in which a culture provides aid in intellectual growth is through a dialogue between the more experienced and the less experienced' (p. 13).

The notion of education taking place within a caring family context is not a new one; Cochin in 1835 described the aims of his school, 'It is to supply the needs, the instructions, the impressions which every child should receive from the presence and examples of his mother' (cited in Blackstone, 1971, p. 16). Hopefully current models of parenting would now include both parents (Harman, 1993). However, the principle of the important role of parents in the care and education of their children has been firmly established (Wolfendale, 1985) and is outlined in this chapter.

Early intervention

In the 1960s, in the USA a great deal of money and effort was spent in developing pre-school educational programmes, in an endeavour to give a better start in life to those children whose achievements in school appeared to be disadvantaged by their home circumstances. An important factor in the more successful programmes appeared to be the mother's direct involvement in the educational process, where mother and child were engaged together in shared activities (Bronfenbrenner, 1975; Ball, 1994). The enduring effects of some of the programmes was attributed to the fact that the key participants, i.e. the mother and child, remained together once the programme was finished, thus ensuring continuity and also benefits for the younger children in the family. Jordan and Powell (1990) described this as a 'transactional process of change' (p. 31), whereby the initial effects on the child cause a change in the child's self esteem and in the parents' (and subsequently the teacher's) view of that child's potential, resulting in a positive spiral that leads to improved life chances for the child.

The supportive adult

In his work with mothers and infants, Bruner (1975; 1977) described the ways in which the mothers helped their children to develop communication skills as a result of a shared activity around an object or event. Identified as particularly important was the way in which mothers provided 'scaffolding' in play. Bruner (1985, cited in Smith, 1993) explained this term as permitting children to do as much as they can by themselves whilst what they cannot do is filled in by the mother's (or other caregiver's) activities; an example might be holding an object of interest, e.g. a brightly coloured musical soft toy for the infant, and moving and repeatedly naming it. Another typical scaffolding activity might be the use of the often repeated phrase 'Up you come', as the infant is taken out of the cot or high chair; a crucial factor being that the act of communication is embedded in a real life context. It is also a multi-dimensional activity involving sight, sound, action and emotion. Thus the child comes to link the spoken words with the action or object, although ultimately the words will be recognized independent of the context.

This framework for understanding children's development stems from Vygotsky (1978); he argued that children could perform much more skilfully with an adult than they could alone; thus until they have acquired competence in developing skills, they require help and supervision (Smith, 1993). Vygotsky refers to a 'zone of proximal development' within which the child and the adult interact and which takes the child on to the next steps of learning (see also Drummond, 1993).

An observation of my daughter Katie aged 3 years 5 months, following a playgroup outing to a National Trust farm provides an example. Katie had bought a postcard to send to her grandmother, her older sister was writing her card at the kitchen table and asked how to spell some words. Katie became enthusiastic about writing her own postcard and wanted me to remind her what we had seen so that she could write it down.

Katie: What did we see?
Mother: Pigs, we saw pigs.
Katie: Yes, and ducks [she makes marks on the card].
Katie: I done that, what else?

She proceeded to make marks on the postcard as we recalled what she had seen. The card was then put into an envelope addressed by me, as Katie had 'written' all over the address space on the card, and it was duly sent off to her grandmother.

Using Vygotsky's framework, but in the context of assessing young children's learning, Drummond (1993) says Vygotsky describes this type of incident as enabling the child to do with assistance today, what she will be able to do by herself tomorrow. In the incident involving Katie, the adult acts as an enabler in the child's learning and the child is seen to be in an apprenticeship role to the adult (Waterland, 1985). He or she is learning alongside the adult (and in this instance an older sister), initially as a spectator, then as a participant, with the adult gradually withdrawing help. In this way considerable meaningful 'tuition' takes place, but without formal teaching.

Donaldson (1984) has written that all normally developing children learn to use and understand speech in the first few years of life without specific instruction; but that a very few seem to do this with reading and writing, stating that the majority don't teach themselves. Donaldson argued that unlike speech, the nature of print is impersonal, citing the example of print on a Coco Pops packet. However, Smith (1984) says that whereas most texts (i.e. print) is not determined by the physical setting in which it is found, some is, e.g. signs and labels. He suggests that in Western cultures this is one way in which children may find their way into literacy.

To return to the Coco Pops example in Chapter 2, written language can become contextualized and personalized, that is related to the emotional and physical situation, by the use to which it is put by the adult (later in the same chapter Donaldson does suggest that environmental print may attract children into reading). Katie's postcard to her grandmother further illustrates this point, in that the writing of it was personally significant for her. To take the example of an adult and child sharing a book together, this often takes place in a close and intimate context. As Taylor and Strickland (1986) write in their book *Family Storybook Reading*, 'Books are like lullabies: They caress a newborn baby, calm a fretful child and help a nervous mother' (p. 23). It is later, within this intimate context and through the support of a sensitive and enabling adult, that the child begins to understand that spoken words emanate from the written page (Campbell, 1992). This process then becomes increasingly 'de-contextualized', i.e. it happens out of familiar settings as the child's experiences of literacy expand in the pre-school and primary school (Donaldson, 1978).

This view of literacy development is supported by Smith (1984), citing Halliday (1975), that children learn about both spoken and written language as they strive to use it, and that they need to see what it will do. As Halliday says, neither will develop in isolation, children are dependent on others to show them. This is particularly true of written language once formal education is under way. In the pre-school years adults can provide this model of literacy within the home setting. However, much learning about literacy will be incidental, that is, not intentionally taught, and will take place within the family.

Parents and literacy

Hannon and James's (1990) interviews about the teaching of reading and writing with the parents of 40 3- and 4-year-olds in Sheffield, showed that not only were the parents interested in their children's pre-school literacy development, but that they spent a great deal of time with their children engaging in reading and writing activities: 'Alongside books and writing materials, parents provided letter games, desks, blackboards, alphabet charts and various other materials to help their children to become literate' (p. 263).

Although not specifically focused upon literacy, Tizard and Hughes (1984) said that one of the strongest impressions gained from their observations of 3- and 4-year-old middle-class and working-class girls and their mothers, was that the children learned from just being with their mothers in an everyday context; writing shopping lists together is cited as one example. This study, amongst others, helps to dispel the myth of the disinterested working-class parent (see also Wells, 1985; Hannon and James, 1990). As Tizard and Hughes noted, writing a shopping list provides a vivid demonstration of the way an everyday activity can engage children in 'literate' experiences. In fact, most of the 'educational' content they recorded took place in the context of an enjoyable game or story.

One aspect of my own study involving 16 parents of 3- and 4-year-old children (Miller, 1992) showed that literacy activities featured strongly in the lives of these children, whose impressive array of skills in this area are detailed in Chapter 2. Questionnaires completed by the parents gave an important, if impressionistic glimpse, into the ways in which literacy was experienced by the children. They were reported to be read to by their parents, almost all on a daily basis; an activity often initiated by the children. All but two parents said they enjoyed this shared activity. Reading and the enjoyment of shared interactions have featured significantly in studies of children who learn to read early (Clark, 1976; Anbar, 1986; Teale, 1986).

A high level of book ownership suggested that the parents valued literacy highly; Wells (1985) found that children who subsequently attained highly in literacy were more likely to possess a large number of their own books. The parents in my study reported a growing interest by the children in a whole range of literacy-based activities, for example, environmental print, words, numbers and emerging writing skills. Imaginative play activities included 'pretend' reading to dollies and teddies, thus showing that the children were learning to behave like a reader (Heath, 1982; Taylor, 1983; Teale, 1986). Parents' reading habits have also been seen to be important in providing models for children (Clark, 1976). All but two of the mothers and over half of the fathers in my study thought they read 'more than average', and there was a high level of library membership amongst the children and their parents. It has been shown that once the habit of using libraries is established, there is a good chance of it persisting until at least the mid-teenage years (Whitehead *et al.*, 1975). In summary, this small-scale study gave an impression of a group of children whose 'roots of literacy' (Goodman, 1984) were being well nurtured by their parents, with subsequent positive outcomes for their literacy development.

A central theme of this book is that the role of parents or other major caregivers is crucial in facilitating, supporting and extending young children's literacy development in the pre-school years. It is suggested that much of this development takes place on a 'moment-to-moment' basis and occurs upon 'the margins of awareness'; that is, without adults being consciously aware that 'instruction' is taking place (Leichter, 1984). It happens as opportunities occur within the context of daily life, and not through the formal teaching of literacy skills. A framework for understanding how these often fleeting interactions can take children forward in their development has been borrowed from Vygotsky (1978).

It would seem that a shared involvement in literacy experiences is already a part of the day-to-day lives of many children and their parents or caregivers (Tizard and Hughes, 1984; Wells, 1985; Miller, 1992). For those parents who are less sure about how best to be involved with their children, their willingness has nevertheless been clearly demonstrated (Hannon and James, 1990). This context for family literacy is a theme which is explored in the next chapter.

CHAPTER 5

Family literacy

In the preface to her book *Family Literacy* Taylor (1983) writes:

> From T-shirts to bubble gum wrappers, children live in a world fashioned in print. Few can escape the abundance of words that fill their homes, and yet we know very little about that world and its effects on learning to read and write in school.

Children who read early

Certain characteristics of the home environment do seem to be important in fostering young children's literacy development; this is hardly surprising as the home is the main setting within which literacy experiences take place in the pre-school years. A key question for both parents and early years educators therefore has to be 'What is it about some home environments that causes differences between children in their literacy development?' In attempting to discover those features which are important, a number of studies have focused upon children who learned to read before formal schooling had begun. One of the most well known of these is Clark's (1976) study of 32 young fluent readers from a variety of home backgrounds. A key feature of these homes seemed to be interested parents who shared in extended and positive spoken interactions with their children; few had been formally taught to read. Older brothers and sisters were important as reading models and 'teachers', and most of the parents and children were library users. The children were described as having a sensitivity to both spoken and written language, and many sources of print seemed to arouse their interest.

This early awareness of, and sensitivity to, books and print, was also identified by Anbar (1986) in her study of six pre-school children from 'middle-class' backgrounds. Her work, like Clark's, was retrospective, that is, based upon parents' recollections of the children's acquisition of early reading skills; therefore a degree of caution is required in interpreting the findings. Memories do not always provide reliable evidence. Only one set of parents recalled having deliberately set out to teach their child to read, yet two of the children were said to be reading unfamiliar picture books and sounding out unfamiliar words at age 34 months.

Anbar said the children went through 'an evolving process of reading acquisition' (p. 73). She identified overlapping steps or stages of development through which the children proceeded. In parallel with this she described the activities which the parents recalled engaging in at various times. For example, each child in the first 12–18 months of life, went through a preliminary period in which they gained a general knowledge about books and print. During this time the children showed interest in books and magazines, e.g. turning the pages, and their parents read to them, often daily. They watched *Sesame Street* and television commercials and played with magnetic letters and alphabet blocks.

This stage phased into a period in which the children acquired letter knowledge and were beginning to recognize some written words. Around 16–25 months of age an interest in the sounds of letters began. 'ABC books, alphabet letters, and a variety of invented sound games were used by the parents' (p. 75). The children then entered a new phase 'making words'. According to the parents, during this time the children were constantly interested in putting words together with their favourite letters, using plastic letters on the fridge, alphabet blocks and cards on the floor or in the sand or 'any other imaginable place' (p. 75).

Following this period, five of the children began to read aloud from familiar books or 'assisted' their parents in reading familiar words; two children began by reading from memory. Anbar's interpretation of this information is that the children were motivated to master the technical skills of reading before they began to read for enjoyment at age 4. However, I think it can be assumed that these children continued to enjoy being read to by their parents, and that the development described went on alongside this, in the context, it would seem, of playful and enjoyable interactions.

More recent studies of young children's literacy development have moved towards observing them in real life situations. However, given the difficulties of intruding upon family life, they not surprisingly often involve the parent as researcher (Bissex, 1980; Lass, 1983; Laminack, 1991). Two key features emerge, firstly, the importance of a supporting and interested adult who is able to respond contingently to the child, i.e. as events occur; secondly, an environment in which the child is able to see the functional meaning of print demonstrated in everyday life. For example, seeing adults writing letters, shopping lists, cheques or using a newspaper to find a television programme. However, a note of caution is needed in interpreting studies which involve the parent as researcher. This is illustrated by Lass's (1983) diary account of her son Jed's developing literacy skills, which she described as somewhat above average. These include a formidable range of abilities, for example being able to recognize 40 words by the age of 2 years. Jed's keenness to read seemed to be a major motivating factor according to Lass, but it is difficult to separate the child's desire to read from the parent's wish for the child to experience success. A degree of tension can be detected as Lass describes Jed's misreading of the word 'hound' for 'Honda', where she describes 'a tug of words' until his tears brought her to her senses. This suggests that intensive studies of one child in 'optimal' conditions for developing literacy should be treated with some caution, in terms of what the more average environment may provide. Nevertheless, such studies can give valuable insights into factors which may contribute to literacy development within the family in pre-school years. The key features would seem to be:

- parents who enjoy interacting with their children in ways which foster literacy development;
- children who either initiate or are responsive to parental interactions;
- an environment in which such experiences are part of everyday life.

The social context of literacy development

The important effect of the child's social setting for literacy development has been highlighted by Heath (1982), in a study of three very different communities in the United States which focused upon literacy-related activities with pre-school children and their parents. 'Maintown' represented what is described as a middle-class school-oriented culture (it should be noted that all the mothers were, or had been, teachers). 'Roadville' was a white mill community and 'Trackton' a black mill rural community. Heath found that children and parents in Maintown interacted together in ways which are very similar to teacher–child interactions in school; for example, parents responding to 'What's that?' questions, discussing the content of books and encouraging children's story telling. Thus, she argued, by the time these children began school they had learned to behave with print in ways which are appropriate for school, and they went on to experience success.

The Roadville and Trackton children did not experience success in school although their families valued this highly. The Roadville community placed great emphasis upon coaching the more formal aspects of literacy. Book reading time focused upon letters of the alphabet, numbers, naming items in picture books and eventually moving on to pre-school workbooks. More informal interactions and conversations around books and print-related material were not encouraged, and events in books and print were not related to real life experiences. For example, when cooking, the written recipe was either not used or not emphasized, thus the child missed the opportunity to link the function of print to a real life event. Although the Roadville children experienced some initial success in school with the more formal aspects of the literacy curriculum, such as knowing the alphabet and recognizing their name, this initial success declined as they were required to become involved in activities which required creativity and independence such as writing a creative story.

Heath found that adults in the Trackton community did not adopt a 'tutoring' role in relation to their children, believing they 'come to know'. Literacy-based items such as books or letter games did not feature in these homes and adults did not sit and read with the children. Features which are a part of the daily routine in many Western settings, such as the bedtime story, did not take place as the children did not have a fixed sleeping routine. Hence, part of the title of Heath's study is 'What no bedtime story means'. When these children began school they faced unfamiliar questions and unfamiliar materials and were unable to take meaning from reading; that is, they had not learned ways of responding which are appropriate for school.

Heath's study emphasized the importance of the context and the culture in which children grow up, arguing that they learn 'ways of taking' (p. 49) meaning from the environment around them, and that this is not a naturally occurring event, but learned behaviour. According to Heath, ways of taking meaning from books and other written material is learned in similar ways to 'eating, sitting, playing games and building houses' (p. 49).

The way in which literacy is influenced by the social context in which young children spend their pre-school years has also been documented by Teale (1986), in his observations of 24 Anglo, black and Mexican pre-school children from low-income families. One of the most striking features of these homes was the way in which literacy was experienced in the context of family and other social events, for example preparations for a family wedding. Little literacy was related to the work of the parents as most were in unskilled or semi-skilled jobs. A great variety of print was found in these homes and most had some writing instruments. There was, however, a considerable range in the amount of literacy experienced by the children. In only three homes was there a special place for writing instruments, so for children wanting to write, paper and pencils were difficult to locate and therefore interest was lost. The importance of adults responding to children's interests in order to support and facilitate their learning has been previously stressed. Just three families engaged in regular story readings and the children in these families had the most highly developed literacy skills.

It is important to note that within this group of families from poor socio-economic circumstances, the children experienced literacy in many different ways, and it should therefore not be assumed that literacy experiences were few or absent. Taylor (1983) supports Teale's (1986) view, that it cannot be assumed that any specific social setting enables children to learn or not to learn about the uses of print, she cites examples of 'middle-class' homes where print is absent and 'working-class' homes littered with print. That is not to say that income levels don't make a difference. As Teale noted, more income means that families have, for example, travel and entertainment opportunities which themselves can facilitate literacy opportunities. The effects of poverty on children's educational opportunities cannot be ignored. Kumar (1993), citing Mack and Lansley (1985) has written:

> Low income means parents have less money to spend on books, educational toys, extra-curricular activities (such as music or sport), or outings to museums, art galleries, cinema, or theatre or a concert, whether organized by the school or at home.
>
> (p. 145)

Kumar goes on to document how the material consequences of poverty such as low income and long hours spent in semi-skilled jobs, can reduce parental motivation and time available to spend with children and to take an active interest in their educational development. Parents of children from minority ethnic groups can be particularly vulnerable, because of their relative lack of knowledge of how the education system works and what their role might be in preparing their children for the more formal aspects of education (Heath, 1984; Gregory, 1992; Kumar, 1993).

It has also been shown that parents' own experiences of literacy, both positive and negative, will affect how literacy is transmitted to their children. Gregory's and Rashid's (1992–3) research demonstrated considerable differences in the literacy learning rates of 5-year-old Bangladeshi children when learning their own written language or the Koran, in a supportive out-of-school context which their parents understood. In this context they made good progress. This contrasted strongly with their poor progress in literacy in the unfamiliar environment of the primary school they attended. In a different context Taylor (1983) described how two fathers in her study who had experienced difficulties in learning to read, were determined to make this a more positive process for their own children. They made it fun to play with print and ensured that the children were not pressurized into 'reading' before they were ready.

According to Taylor (1986), the reason why some children fail to have success with literacy is because they don't have what she describes as incidental 'moment-to-moment' experiences with print (illustrated by Katie in the first chapter of this book). She suggests that the most significant transmission of literacy within families occurs through the use of written language in the ongoing life of the family. This in turn will affect how children view and use literacy in their own lives. However, studies such as Heath's (1984), Teale's (1986), and Gregory and Rashid's (1992–3) indicate that there needs to be an understanding about differences in previous literacy experiences and cultural practices if children are to build upon what they bring to more formal educational settings. To give a personal example of this, my own children, when young, described my job as 'writing' as that is what they observed me do a lot at home. Thus, a great deal of 'office' and writing play took place in their early lives; paper, writing implements, including a computer for word processing, were readily available to them. This is the 'transmission' process in practice. Older children in the family can make an important contribution to this process. I recorded an incident in which my daughters Chloe and Katie, then aged 9 and 6, were playing schools. This involved the younger child's knowledge of the alphabet being thoroughly checked out; as Taylor says, they shape each others' literacy experiences.

The key features of family literacy which influence children's development in reading and writing are summarized by Teale (1986) as:

- young children and adults (or older brothers and sisters) being involved together in interactions around literacy;
- children's independent opportunities for exploring written language;
- observations of others using written language.

These are encompassed within three broad categories which condition children's literacy experiences within the family, proposed by Leichter (1984):

The physical environment

This includes the level of economic or educational resources (and I would add cultural practices).

Interpersonal interaction

Opportunities for incidental interactions centred on literacy with parents, brothers and sisters and the level of visual stimulation relating to print, e.g. writing created in the home such as notes and shopping lists. (It is suggested that the contents of the wastepaper basket can provide an insight into the level of literacy in the home.)

The emotional/motivational climate

Emotional relationships within the family, including parents' own positive and negative recollections of experiences with literacy and also the aspirations of family members.

Linking home and pre-school

It has been suggested in this chapter that the cultural, social and emotional climate of the home all have a part to play in the development of literacy in the pre-school years. Heath's (1982) study demonstrated how, as a result of these inter-connecting factors, some children arrive at school more prepared for the experiences offered than others. Therefore, the pre-school or primary school has a part to play in supporting those children who are less well prepared for literacy in these more formal settings; however, it seems that just the opposite can occur.

Tizard and Hughes (1984) recorded conversations of mother–daughter pairs over one afternoon at home, some of which were focused around literacy activities. They then recorded the children on two mornings in the pre-schools they attended. They found the 'working-class' girls gave a misleading impression of their language abilities, which in turn caused the adults working with them to simplify their language and ask less challenging questions of them. Parallels can be seen here with the 'Trackton' children in Heath's (1982) study and the children of the Bangladeshi community studied by Gregory and Rashid (1992–3). Thus, it is possible to see how a 'chicken and egg' situation can arise, where a child who is less comfortable and less confident in a more formal setting containing unfamiliar adults and unfamiliar materials, receives a reduced rather than an enriched input because of the way in which they present to the adult. A long-term study by Wells (1985) which followed 128 children from their pre-school years through to secondary school supports this view. Wells claimed it is the unfamiliar context and unfamiliar materials encountered in pre-school or school which can disadvantage children whose family literacy does not reflect the literacy encountered in school. This suggests that professional educators need to start where children are in terms of cultural or social background. In doing so they will be ascribing value to the literacy of the family and the contribution which each child brings to the pre-school or school.

CHAPTER 6

Sharing books in the pre-school: what children learn

Children and adults sharing books together in the pre-school years is a key feature of family literacy. A history of being read to features strongly in the lives of children who have learned to read before formal schooling begins, or who subsequently achieve well in this area (Clark, 1976; Heath, 1982; Lass, 1983; Taylor, 1983; Payton, 1984; Anbar, 1986; Teale, 1986; Wells, 1987). It was shown by Wells (1985) that listening to stories read aloud is significantly related to children's knowledge about literacy on entry to school and to their later reading achievement. Smith (1985) and Clay (1977) have said that being read to enables children to learn about concepts relating to print. Therefore, there appears to be a general agreement among researchers that 'reading to pre-school children is a good thing; it is an activity through which children may develop interest and skill in literacy' (Teale, 1981, p. 902).

Encouraging book sharing between children and their parents is a key feature of a number of pre-school parental involvement projects outlined in Chapter 7. However, as Teale (1981) has pointed out, much of the research on reading to children tells us little about how and why it affects literacy development. He therefore highlighted the need for studies of children and parents sharing books together in real life settings, in order to clarify what happens during this activity and what the consequences are for literacy development. He elaborated 'reading is not a seamless whole' (Teale, 1984, p. 113), saying that we need to know more about the nature of the activity we call story reading. Sharing books in the pre-school years and its implications for young children's literacy development is explored in this chapter.

Sharing books: the role of the adult

From the very earliest months of life the role of the adult is crucial in demonstrating to the infant what books do and what you can do with them.

What makes the pre-school period such a rich and exciting time, is that there are countless odd moments throughout the day when opportunities for literacy can occur, particularly in settings in and around the home. Joint activities with books may begin with the brightly coloured and eminently chewable sponge and plastic books which may be a regular feature of bath time; such books are readily available in chain stores and supermarkets. Initially the baby may mouth, chew, splash with and generally explore the book with all the senses; eventually the interaction will change to focusing upon the book and the features therein. This will provide an early opportunity for the adult to turn the pages, to talk about the pictures and point to the words as the story is told or read. Children's first books, often made from durable material such as cloth and cardboard, will allow for similar explorations, until the adult enables the child to move on by demonstrating, in playful situations, what else you can do with books.

Despite the fact that mothers have different ways of interacting around books with their young children, i.e. what researchers call different 'teaching styles'; routine interactions with books seem to provide children with the basic rules for learning about literacy. According to Snow and Nino (1986) these involve learning that:

- books are for reading, not manipulating;
- the book is the focus of the interaction;
- pictures represent objects or events;
- pictures are for naming, i.e they elicit a word, a skill later transferred to reading;
- book events occur outside real time;
- books constitute a fictional world (which my younger daughter used to clarify by asking 'Is it in the real world?') (see also Snow *et al.*, 1985).

The importance of the adult as a model for literacy acts, whether a parent, other caregiver or professional educator, has been emphasized in previous chapters. Although exploring the role of the teacher in developing children's reading and writing skills in the earliest years of school, Geekie and Raban (1993) draw upon a study by Nino and Bruner (1978) which also looked at the ways in which mothers engaged in remarkably similar and familiar routines with their infants when sharing books with them. These routines contained what are described as 'formats' which created a predictable structure which made it easier for the child to learn. An example is given of a typical book-sharing interaction containing just four key utterances:

1. an attentional vocative (Look!);
2. a query (What's that?);
3. a label (It's a horse);
4. feedback (Yes).

To quote Geekie and Raban (1993, p. 19):

> the adults first try to establish joint attention. They then make the children aware that there is a standard vocalization which 'stands' for the referent and then provide feedback that tells the children whether they have provided an appropriate response.

So, the adult draws the child's attention to the picture, poses a question about it, receives a response from the child, praises and confirms. In audio tape recordings of five 3- and 4-year-olds with their mothers, in what were agreed as typical story reading sessions, I found such patterns were identifiable. Ross and his mother follow very similar formats as they embark upon a story about a football match. Firstly, Ross's mother establishes joint attention by using a query about the picture:

Mother: Who can you see Ross, who's that?
Ross: Mmm, don't know.
Mother: That's Mungo.
Ross: Mungo, with the ball?
Mother: That's right.

Although Ross is initially unable to supply the correct response, i.e. the label, his mother models this for him, then confirms his second response with her feedback 'That's right.' Such an activity, repeated many times with remarkable similarity, provides a predictable and supportive framework for coming to know about books; that is what they are for and what you do with them. This framework focuses the child's attention on to the 'event' on the page. Geekie and Raban make the point that once naming is routinely achieved by the child, the adult moves the child on into a new zone of proximal development (Vygotsky, 1978), where it is learned that naming the picture is a prerequisite to commenting on and talking about it, thus moving on to the next step of learning. There is a shift from labelling objects to discussing events, and predicting what might happen before or afterwards (Snow and Nino, 1986). To return to Ross and his mother – Josh, who is the main character in the book, is with his twin sister Jessie who is about to spill some water she is carrying:

Mother: What's happening here, look.
Ross: Don't know.
Mother: What's she got in her hand?
Ross: Don't know.
Mother: Look, what do you think's happened?
Ross: Mmm – water.
Mother: Yes, and she's spilt it, hasn't she?
Ross: Mmm.

So, Ross is invited to predict what will happen to the water and when he is unable to do this, he is supported by his mother who draws his attention to

Jessie's hand. A similar sequence can be seen as Katie and her mother share *The Witch Baby* by Wendy Smith (1987). Wanda the witch baby is making unsuccessful attempts to cast her first spell. In the following sequence she is attempting to fly from a wall in the garden:

Mother: Where's she going to go Katie, look.
Katie: I don't know.
Mother: You have a look, where does she go?
Katie: Fell on. I don't know what she fell on.
Mother: Fell on the floor didn't she?

This type of interaction has been described by Bruner (1977) as a 'scaffolding dialogue' between mother and child, which enables the child's participation in the event with the support of the adult. Support is gradually reduced by the adult, dependent either upon the age of the child or familiarity with the books involved (Snow and Nino, 1986). Contributions from the adult, such as comments or questions about the story appear to decrease with repeated readings. Phillips and McNaughton (1990) audio taped ten middle-class New Zealand parents with their pre-school children in repeated story reading situations and found that as they became more familiar with the story the children took over, clarifying and anticipating what was being read.

Geekie and Raban (1993) go on to make interesting links between such parent–child interactions with learning in school, where the teacher observed by them used a similar standard framework for interacting with the 4- and 5-year-olds in literacy lessons. Familiar routines and strategies were established by Rhonda, the teacher, which the children could eventually draw upon to support their own learning. For example, she involved them in a game of finding letters and words from notices around the classroom, these were eventually used by the children to support their attempts at independent writing, to quote 'The patterns of exchange formerly used by Rhonda have now become the property of the children' (p. 70).

This insight of Geekie and Raban's offers a useful pointer to the ways in which some continuity can be provided from the pre-school into school, particularly for the youngest children. As they state, familiar adults need to be sensitive to what children are able to do, know and understand so that they can raise their expectations and adjust their interactions according to the child's growing abilities.

Social and cultural differences

It would, however, be a mistake to assume, as Teale (1981) has said, that reading to children is a seamless whole; in other words, that all children benefit from the ways of interacting described on previous pages. As seen in Chapter 5, it is not the same sort of experience for all children, in that adult–child interactions around literacy events can differ according to culture and social circumstance. The work of Heath (1982) has shown how the 'mainstream' or middle-class families in her study interacted in ways which bore remarkable similarities to teacher–child interactions in school; thus advantaging the children concerned. Ross and his mother, from my own research, provide an example of this; the story is barely under way before the type of interaction described by Heath begins:

Mother: This is Josh, he is mad about football. He has a naughty little sister called Trixie and a twin sister called Jessie. Mungo, his dog, likes to play with his new football.
Who can you see Ross, who's that?
Ross: Mmm. I don't know.
Mother: That's Mungo.
Ross: Mungo, with the ball?
Mother: That's right, and which one is the one who likes football? Which one's Josh?
[It is assumed Ross points.]
That's right.
And which one's his twin sister?
[It is assumed Ross points.]
Very good.
What's happening here – look.
Ross: Don't know.
Mother: What's she got in her hand?
Ross: Don't know.

This questioning continued for two more pages of transcription before returning to the story. Story times with Ross seem to be treated with some seriousness by his mother. The tape recording ends with her saying 'It is quarter to three in the afternoon now. We sometimes sit down and we read a story or we do some counting or the alphabet before we pick Samantha up from school.' In comparison, tape recordings of another child, Christopher and his mother show far fewer interruptions.

Heath (1982) draws attention to such differences when describing the working-class community of Roadville, where despite the bright and stimulating early environment featuring 'literacy-based stimuli' (p. 57), and reading-related bedtime activities, Roadville children experienced difficulty in achieving literacy in school. Heath linked this to the ways in which the children experienced books. Interactions which were cooperative and which involved the participation of both child and adult were discouraged in favour of 'learning' from the material in the book. The Trackton children, from a poor black community, experienced an environment described as 'almost entirely human' (p. 64). Reading materials were absent and bedtime did not have any special routine, such as a bedtime story.

Although older children in the family made attempts at literacy-based play, this was not encouraged by adults. In school Trackton children face demands for unfamiliar questions and explanations, for example being asked to identify and name items in books, which bear no resemblance to the real item. The kinds of questions asked about books were unfamiliar to these children, resulting in them being unable to interact with print and print-related material in ways which are necessary for school success. Most subsequently did not achieve well in school and eventually stopped trying.

It is important, however, for professional educators not to make negative assumptions about families who experience literacy in different ways. Gregory and Rashid (1992–3) in their work with Bangladeshi families warn against this. They point out that many 'non-school oriented' families have their own literacy practices and methods of initiating children into these practices, which contrast sharply with practices expected of children when they enter school. Frequent story reading sessions were observed in the homes studied by Gregory and Rashid, but many parents were unable to share books with their children because of their unfamiliar nature, in this case school reading-scheme books. It would seem that the nature and format of book-sharing sessions between children and adults can either advantage or disadvantage children when they enter the more formal setting of pre-school centres. This places a burden of responsibility upon the shoulders of professional educators and others working with young children, to provide imaginative and meaningful ways of building upon the existing knowledge and experience of children in their care.

Book knowledge and concepts about print

It would be a great help to parents and professional educators to know exactly which features of story book reading help children to develop into skilled and enthusiastic readers. There have been attempts by researchers to capture identifiable features in order to link specific practices with specific literacy outcomes, however, it would seem that the outcomes are more easily identified than the practices which bring them about.

A knowledge of concepts about print has been seen as one outcome (Clay, 1977) and is detailed in Chapter 2. In a review of research about early literacy development, Goodman (1984) concluded that the ability to handle books seemed a universal skill for the 3–5 year-olds studied. They had also learned that print, not pictures, carried the message and were able to demonstrate an understanding of terms such as 'read', 'page' and 'story', if asked 'show me' questions. In a nine month long book-sharing project, described in Chapters 2 and 7, in which 31 pre-school children and their parents were encouraged to share books together on a regular basis, I found that the children's knowledge about books and print concepts had increased. Whilst acknowledging that factors such as age and maturation have a part to play in children's development, it seemed reasonable to conclude that specific knowledge such as knowing what writing is and knowing that a left page is read before a right, had come about as a result of familiarity with books; probably as a result of parents and other adults modelling and pointing out these features (Miller, 1992).

In attempting to take a close look at the kinds of information children tend to focus upon during story readings and the nature and frequency of their questions, Yaden *et al.* (1989) audio taped seven 3- and 4-year-olds at home in different settings and with different books. They found that a general pattern emerged. Most questions were about the pictures, story meaning and word meaning; questions about the writing occurred least, although a wide variety of questions were noted relating to characters, letters, authors and the act of reading itself. Such a small-scale study can only offer a 'discerning description' of what happens in real life story readings, as the authors acknowledged. Nevertheless, they believe their work supports Well's (1987) findings, that story readings provide a breadth of information about how written language works and what it does.

If we return to the notion of literacy development having roots which are nurtured and fed by pre-school experiences (see Goodman, 1984 in Chapter 2), it is possible to see the part that sharing books with a familiar adult may play. Books can allow the adult to demonstrate the functions and forms of literacy, that is, what writing in books does and the forms it can take. Christopher's mother demonstrates this as she begins the story about Barclay:

Mother: Right, what's this book called?
Christopher: [unintelligible].
Mother: No it's not, it's called *The Circus,* he's in a circus though isn't he? It's called . . . ? Barclay – that's the name of the dog isn't it?

This strategy of drawing Christopher's attention to the title and linking it into the book is used by his mother in other recordings, so it seems reasonable to assume that eventually Christopher will come to know that books have titles and that these give a clue as to what the book is about. In this way, during story readings, the adult can also use oral language about written language (Goodman, 1984), using, for example, terms such as 'title', 'author', 'word', 'letter' or 'read'.

Identifying meaning in the text and life to text experiences

Despite the fact that somehow some children gain a detailed knowledge about books and print in the pre-school years, studies of children and adults sharing books in natural settings such as the home, show that the focus of the book sharing is almost exclusively upon the process of identifying meaning in the stories read and not upon features such as the words, letters or the direction of the print. In an attempt to take a closer look at regular story book readings in a home setting, Phillips and McNaughton (1990) audio taped ten middle-class New Zealand parents with their preschool children in repeated story reading situations. The main focus seemed to be upon identifying what the story was about. Both parents and children made more comments about the story rather than the print itself.

Observations of mothers with their 4-year-old daughters at home showed how through their questions, the 4-year-old girls attempted to 'get at the meaning' of the story. Mothers would often clarify by relating the text and pictures to the children's experience, or would take the opportunity to expand their general knowledge (Tizard and Hughes, 1984).

To return to my own audio tape recordings, Christopher and his mother are reading a book about Barclay, a circus dog who has wandered off from the circus having grown too old for his act and is looking for food. Chrisptopher's mother takes the opportunity to talk about the role of the dustman.

Mother: He saw a bone in a dustbin.
Christopher: Mummy.
Mother: There it is, see.
Christopher: A two.
Mother: But someone took it away. He's the dustman isn't he?
Christopher: Yeh.
Mother: Tipping all the rubbish into the big dustcart.

In an extract from a reading of *The Witch Baby* (Smith, 1987) shared by Katie and her mother, a similar pattern can be seen. Throughout the story there are no references to the written features of the text, questions relate mainly to clarifying aspects of the story and there are plenty of 'text to life' references; that is, how the child's life experiences are linked to the story by the adult (Gregory, 1992). In the story Wanda the witch baby is visiting her Granny, and Katie attempts to clarify who Granny is in the book. Katie's grandmother, who is disabled, had just been to stay and the 'life to text' reference seems to arouse Katie's concern about how she would manage on her return home. The brackets show attempts to take Katie back to the story.

Katie: Is that her Granny?
Mother: Yes, our Granny has just been to stay hasn't she?
Katie: Why has she gone home?
Mother: Well because she has to go back to see to her house.
Katie: Why?

Mother: Well because she's got lots of things to do, she's got to do the cleaning hasn't she, get her shopping and she wants to see Uncle Fran.
[You may care to try.]
[Wanda was very glad that she had come to see Granny.]
Katie: She can't go without us.
Mother: We'll go and see her at Christmas time won't we?
Katie: But she can't go without us.
Mother: Why?
Katie: Because, umh, she get lost.
Mother: Well Daddy took her home, got her safely home.
Katie: Who will take her?
Mother: Daddy took her home in the car.
Katie: Who took, who took her, who can take her to the – her shopping to take . . . ?
Mother: Uncle Fran will take her shopping in his car.
Right.
['Thank you for the tea and all your help' she said 'And now please do your going home spell.']

Thus, Gregory suggests (1992) the adult shows how 'life experiences can be brought to bear on the text' (p. 39). One way in which this type of strategy may assist children when encountering book sharing in pre-school centres, is that they have learned an interpretation of what 'reading lessons' in school are about. For children from 'non-school oriented backgrounds', Gregory suggests, school reading may have little meaning. Therefore, she argues, these children require a more conscious teaching of what reading in more formal educational settings is about.

Re-readings

The common activity of re-reading a familiar book to children has aroused the attention of researchers and appears to serve an important function. For example, children will often correct their parents if they deviate from the story as written, and will attempt to 'read' a familiar book themselves or to dolls or pets (Robinson and Sulzby, 1984, cited in Cornell *et al.*, 1988; Miller, 1992). Taylor and Strickland (1986) observed parents in their homes playing the game of 'reading stories silly' as they changed the wording of books to 'outrageous dialogues that only the child and parent can understand' (p. 61). This strategy alerts children to the story line and gives them the opportunity to think critically about a text they know well; they can join in the reading and invent new variations. I have seen teachers in school use a similar strategy, that of deliberately mis-reading words or sentences to draw children's attention to a familiar story reading.

Re-readings are important in that children learn alongside the skilled adult to behave like a reader; they see themselves as part of what Smith (1985) calls 'the literacy club' (p. 134). In other words, there is an expectation on the part of the children and the supporting adults, that they will eventually become readers. As Jonathan, one 4-year-old in my book-sharing project confidently said to me when we were sharing a book together, 'You just start me off, then I'll be able to read it' (Miller, 1992, p. 118).

To return to my audio recordings. One set of tapes featuring two young sisters sharing books with their mother was extremely difficult to analyse, as the girls 'read' and recalled obviously familiar stories almost simultaneously with their mother, amidst much giggling and evident enjoyment. Katie, towards the end of *The Witch Baby* is prompted to recall an event from a previous reading.

Katie: He's turned a witch into a snake.
Mother: Oh, that's a good trick isn't it, a good spell? . . . the simple and foolproof spell that her grandmother had taught her. Come out, come out all you animals with tails and dance. But not one animal appeared.
And what happened though?
Katie: The sun got pink.
Mother: Mmh. The moon turned pink.

Children as young as 1 and 2 years of age have been observed using the expressions and content of stories which had been repeatedly read to them, in their subsequent play with puppets. This suggests that re-reading familiar texts may aid the skills of retrieval and recall (Snow *et al.*, 1985). Interestingly these skills appear to be affected by the type and content of the book, for example in an experimental situation it was found that the content of narrative rather than alphabetic books were more likely to be recalled (Cornell *et al.*, 1988).

Story language

There is no doubt that children learn about the language of stories such as 'once upon a time' by having stories read to them (Mandel-Morrow, 1988). The evidence for this is beautifully documented by Wolf, the mother of two young girls and Heath (1992) in their book *The Braid of Literature*, in which nine years of book sharing are recorded and analysed. The book documents how literature pervades the life of this family, both parents having shared books with their daughters throughout many opportunities within their daily lives. A bathtime event illustrates 3-year-old Lindsey's use of story language, where she is playing with a yellow sponge and a rubber frog; she tells her mother that she is playing 'The Frog Prince'. Lindsey, as the princess, weeps into her hands and asks in the frog's croaky voice 'What's the matter, Princess?' In a 'princess's' voice Lindsey says 'I've lost my golden ball.' Replying as the frog she says 'I'll get it, but you must promise to let me sleep on your fine silk pillow' (p. 83). As her mother notes, Lindsey was able to apply story language to life as well as to books.

Fox (1994) recently captivated an audience of early years educators as she played, and spoke about, tape recorded stories told by five pre-school children over a number of years; the children having been selected on the basis of their extensive experiences with books. With the help of their parents she traced the origins of many of the stories to books previously shared and read, and showed how the written structures of stories were used in the children's oral language. The following is an extract from 5-year-old Josh's story: 'One sunny morning little Joshua was awake he found in his bedroom marvellous presents he put them by his side and showed them to his mother "Oh" he cried "It's Christmas . . ."' (Fox, 1992). As she goes on to say 'the sound of book language is very clear' (p. 9). It is also pertinent to this book to note that all the children in her study were fluent readers and writers at the age of 7. Children can only develop such knowledge from experiencing books with adults. We have to ask ourselves, how else they can learn all this?

Time for stories

In many families sharing books together is perhaps one of the few aspects of literacy for which specific time is created. In their book *Family Storybook Reading* Taylor and Strickland (1986) described book sharing across a diverse range of families. They say, 'For many families, storybook sharing is such a natural part of daily life that parents rarely spend much time actually planning it or reflecting upon its value. They simply do it' (p. 33). It has, however, been suggested in the previous chapter that the way in which family literacy is experienced and organized may differ according to the cultural, social and economic status of the family (Heath, 1982; Teale, 1986; Gregory, 1992). Only three families out of 24 in Teale's (1986) study engaged the 2- and 3-year-olds in regular story times, literacy was experienced mainly in other situations which were primarily of a social nature; for example in preparing for a wedding reception which involved writing lists and invitations. It was found that the children who had experienced regular story reading were the most highly developed in relation to emerging literacy skills.

Ten mainstream (middle-class) parents in a New Zealand study were asked to keep a diary for 28 days of all story book readings to see if it was 'an established social practice' (Phillips and McNaughton, 1990, p. 198). The diaries showed that half the families read to their children primarily at bedtime and the other half at any time during the day, thus book readings, predominantly with story books, formed a regular and substantial part of family life.

In my own study, 14 of the 16 parents of the 3- and 4-year-olds who completed a questionnaire about literacy in the home, said that they read to their children daily for around 10 to 15 minutes. Bedtime proved to be the most popular time and was named as a special time by 14 of the parents, the remaining 2 citing lunchtime (after playgroup had ended) or anytime during the day (Miller, 1992). When observing 4-year-old girls and their mothers at home in the daytime, Tizard and Hughes (1984) did not see a large number of story sessions, suggesting that books and stories were linked with bedtime. Stories were often suggested by the mothers when the children became tired and fractious; they say 'Perhaps for this reason, story times were rarely the cosy, idyllic occasions traditionally portrayed in the media' (p. 58). It has been argued by Heath (1982) that the bedtime story is 'a major literacy event' which is a focus of lives of mainstream (i.e. middle-class) families, yet she believes that few parents are consciously aware of its importance for the kinds of 'learning and displays of knowledge expected in school' (p. 51).

A cautionary note

A crucial question in a discussion about the importance of sharing books with young children in the pre-school years, is whether it will ensure later success in reading in the conventional sense. There is no doubt that for many young children, sharing books with adults in the pre-school years provides a grounding for, and insight into, what reading is about once they enter more formal educational settings; thus providing them with a good start (Gregory, 1992). However, as Wolf and Heath (1992) discuss in the Epilogue to their book; what is described as 'The comparatively stripped down life of learning to read and write in school' (p. 191), may in fact disadvantage children for whom literacy has been about discussing and interpreting rich and varied story books. To quote, 'Opportunities to talk about and act out stories do not guarantee that children will become smooth decoders' (p. 191). The example is given of Wolf's daughter, Lindsey, who despite her vast and rich experience with books had difficulty with decoding print. As the authors say, she well understood the purpose which print served, but could not 'unlock' the patterns of print on starting school. This implies a need to take account of individual differences in children, as Lindsey's sister Ashley had shown an interest in 'what letters said', from an early age (p. 192). An additional factor to consider is personality differences between children. For Lindsey reading was a social act and she disliked reading alone.

Summary

For many children, sharing books with a familiar adult seems to play an important part in fostering early literacy development. Sharing books with parents or familiar adults provides a 'tutorial' context within which, for the majority of children, important knowledge about literacy is acquired, albeit, in ways which are different for each child. What is less certain is which specific practices foster which skills.

It would seem that a great deal of knowledge about print and books is acquired 'incidentally', that is, not specifically taught. For some children there may be more pressure from the adult to focus upon particular features of books, such as recognizing words and letters. Some studies of children who learn to read before formal schooling begins would tend to support this view. Individual characteristics of children will also have an influence upon the context within which literacy is acquired; what is less clear is whether, for example, the quest for information on the part of the child is an outcome of previous literacy experiences, or whether it is a response to a facilitating literacy environment. The studies reviewed in this chapter suggest it is probably a combination of the two.

A problem for researchers is that it is difficult to capture the essence of what is, as Taylor (1986) describes, 'an intimate occasion that cannot be staged' (p. 19). She says that the sharing of books between parents and children is intimate and personally constructed and therefore not a situation that a researcher can easily emulate. Stories are embedded in families' personal histories, thus allowing children to integrate them into their own experience (Tizard and Hughes, 1984; Taylor, 1986; Fox, 1992). Research techniques can be intrusive of family life and less intrusive methods, such as audio tape recordings, fail to record important visual information, such as the adult pointing to the words as the story is read.

In this chapter I have argued that adults and children sharing books together in the pre-school years is established as an important part of early literacy development for many children. In the earliest stages very young children may learn what a book is and that it is handled differently to other objects. Books then become a focal point for labelling objects and events and relating these to the child's experience. The quest for meaning in the text is a key feature of children's questions about books and provides adults with the opportunity to offer important information about characters, authors, titles, story lines and features of the text. The evidence suggests that in many homes parents are providing their young children with opportunities for sharing books and may only require assurance that they are doing the right thing (Hannon and James, 1990). For such families additional opportunities for book sharing will be a bonus; for others who may benefit from additional support, a book-sharing project such as those described in the next chapter, may be one way of providing this.

CHAPTER 7

Parents as partners: setting up a literacy project

> Somehow we need to bridge the gap between home and school so that reading in one is reading in the other.
>
> (Taylor, 1982, p. 548)

The case was made in the previous chapter that children and adults sharing books together in the pre-school years has a positive effect upon children's literacy development. Evidence was offered that sharing books is an activity which many parents of young children include as part of their daily routine, in which case additional opportunities for book sharing would be an added enrichment. It was also suggested that for others additional support or encouragement might facilitate this important activity.

Projects involving parents in the development of their pre-school children's literacy skills has been an area of developing interest. Weinberger *et al.* (1990) suggest that this reflects the change in the way that literacy development is being seen. Whereas the teaching of literacy skills was once viewed as the exclusive province of the school, there is now a growing recognition of the wealth of information young children acquire from being with adults in the pre-school years, as noted in Chapters 4 and 5. The ways in which this can be encouraged and developed in the context of parent–professional partnership is the focus of this chapter.

A review of literacy projects

In setting out on a new venture it can be helpful to learn from others. A review of some recent projects, based mainly in the United Kingdom, revealed a wide and varying range of approaches, describing ways in which parents have been assisted and enabled to participate in their children's literacy development in the pre-school years. A description of some of these projects follows in order to demonstrate their range and diversity.

The Calderdale Pre-school Parent–Book Project (Griffiths and Edmonds, 1988)

This project attempted to extend parental involvement in reading into two nursery units in a social priority area and lasted for approximately nine months. Books were borrowed on a weekly basis and parents made comments about the book, or their child's reaction to it, on a record card. This took place on a specific day to enable parent–teacher discussion. Impetus was maintained through the use of video material involving a parent–child story reading and 'sticky badges' for the children. Some outcomes are worth noting:

- Parents seemed to be spending more time in shared activities with their children.
- Project books replaced TV and cartoon books as children's favourites.
- Parents talked more positively about reading with their children.
- Parents felt that their children's language skills had improved.
- Two of the 17 parents found it easier to talk to the teachers.
- The results from the *Concepts about Print Test* (Clay, 1979) showed increases in literacy skills for the project group and decreases for two comparison groups.
- Parents made many positive comments on the record cards about the books and their children's responses to them.
- Both parents and teachers wished to continue and extend the project.

Share-a-Story sessions (Weinberger, 1988)

Jo Weinberger was the teacher of a 60-place nursery class in Sheffield at the time of the project and wished to discover whether parents wanted to be involved in aspects of their pre-school children's reading development. Two events spread over a series of days and evenings concerned with reading were arranged. These included a Share-a-Story session involving parents reading with their children in the nursery and participating in reading-related activities in specially set up story areas. This was followed by a meeting to discuss how reading was approached in the nursery. It was found that parents were willing to become involved in reading activities with their children; around 50 per cent of parents attended the sessions and were said to be genuinely interested in the project. It was viewed by Jo Weinberger as a useful starting point for home–school links.

A Head Start to Learning: Workshop 4 (Currie and Bowes, 1988)

The project initiators, Currie and Bowes were based in the school psychological service and learning support service in Strathclyde. The workshop described was one of a series of four pilot workshops aimed at various aspects of children's development. It involved parents whose children had no nursery experience and who would eventually attend a local primary school situated in an educational priority area. This project is included here because it contains some of the less desirable features of the 'Transplant Model' of working with parents (Mittler and Mittler, 1982), characterized by the professionals' view of themselves as experts transplanting their skills and knowledge on to parents, without taking account of the parents as contributors to the partnership.

Parents were 'interviewed' by the headteacher to explain the aims of the workshops. Content was decided upon on the basis of a formal assessment of each child to identify 'areas of need'. The workshop described took place on one afternoon and was based in the local library. It featured an introduction to story telling; discussion and demonstration centred around choosing books, looking at pictures and asking questions. A book was raffled as a prize. The outcome seems worth quoting:

> Our assumption that these parents would be most in need of guidance was proved wrong, as half of our parent group were well motivated, interested parents who were naturally stimulating their children using many of the methods used in the workshops. For many of these parents the greatest benefit was an explanation of why their involvement was beneficial to their child.
>
> (1988, p. 199)

Currie and Bowes go on to say that they felt they should have targeted all parents; subsequently follow-up meetings/workshops were organized for all the parents of children in the first class of the infant school.

Workshops or projects based on assumptions about 'disadvantaged' children and their parents have been seriously questioned (Wells, 1985; Tizard and Hughes, 1984). There is a danger in offering parents what professionals think they need, rather than what parents actually want. The value of Currie and Bowes workshop would seem to be in reassuring parents that they were 'doing the right things' with their children, and offering ideas for extending these activities where needed.

Sharing stories: parents involvement in reading with inner-city children (Robson and Whitley, 1989)

Robson and Whitley, two lecturers based at Northumbria University aimed their project at 44 children and their parents based in a nursery class attached to an inner-city primary school, in an educational priority area. The project lasted for one school year and aimed to encourage parents to read regularly to their pre-school children. Parents were encouraged to borrow up to two picture/story books to read to their children at home on a weekly basis. These were purchased from a university research fund. Record cards were kept by the parents to record their own and the children's opinions of the books. Formal testing showed no significant difference in reading achievement, although parental interest remained high throughout the project.

Robson and Whitley speculate that what they describe as disappointing results may be due to a number of factors, such as the input being too little and too late. Another factor may be the limitations of the formal testing of reading skills in very young children, as discussed in Chapter 1, which may not demonstrate what they have achieved.

The Nursery Book-Share Project (Cooper, 1987)

Judith Cooper's six-week initiative stemmed from a change in admissions policy which resulted in children staying in her 40-place nursery class for one extra term. As nursery policy did not include the formal introduction to reading which these children would have experienced on entry to school, parents expressed concern that they would 'get behind with their reading'. Judith Cooper was also concerned that some children were forming negative attitudes towards reading, announcing that they 'couldn't read'. Her project was intended to focus upon parents' interests and anxieties in relation to their children's reading development and to provide a resource bank of books to borrow.

A preliminary meeting was held to assess parental interest and to establish a mutually acceptable way of operating. Books, obtained from Penguin pulp stock, were exchanged at the end of each morning and afternoon session. Record cards were kept to record the number of books read and to allow for parents' comments. When possible children were invited to share borrowed books with the class teacher. A diary of events was maintained by the class teacher over the trial period, and both teacher and parents commented on record cards to obtain information about the children's approaches to books. There were also informal discussions with parents. Over half of the families in the nursery class were represented and all these parents were positive about the continuation of the project. Children were felt to be more positive in their view of themselves as emerging readers and after an enthusiastic beginning book borrowing averaged out to one book a week for each child.

The Nursery Library Project (Gaines, 1988)

Keith Gaines, a special needs advisory support teacher in Castleford, established tape/story libraries in two nursery units, resourced by the schools library service. Books were recorded on to cassettes for parents and children to borrow. Evaluation involved interviews with the children about reading, and assessment on Clay's *Concepts about Print Test* (1979). Interesting differences emerged between borrowers and non-borrowers; the borrowers scoring half as much again on the literacy test after a six-month period. The project has since been extended to other schools, largely resourced by parents' fundraising activities. Teachers whose nursery schools were involved reported that children were more ready to read, and that younger siblings entered the units with the expectation of borrowing the books and tapes, thus approaching reading with a more positive set of expectations.

Literacy newsletters (Taylor and Walls, 1990)

This project, set in a kindergarten in New Hampshire, America, is included because it seemed an interesting and different approach to improving home–school communication about early literacy development. The teacher, Leigh Walls, sent home regular newsletters to parents relating to emergent literacy theory, but explained in an 'everyday' way; sometimes with accompanying articles. This was followed up by writing to the parents suggesting ways in which they might help their child to become literate. For example, suggesting books they might enjoy at home and describing some of the things the children had been doing in school. Individual parent conferences were held, focusing around the child's literacy development. Leigh Walls claimed that as a result, a strong working relationship had developed with parents.

The Share-a-Book Scheme (Miller, 1992)

The Share-a-Book Scheme was a book-borrowing scheme set in a pre-school playgroup which aimed to encourage parents to share books with their children on a regular basis. The organization of the scheme was planned collaboratively with the playgroup staff. Books were displayed in an area adjacent to the main room used by the playgroup and a record card system was maintained for each child by the playgroup staff, containing details of books and dates borrowed. Three borrowing times were established at the end of the playgroup morning. Parents were given a leaflet containing information about the scheme and suggestions for sharing books. A termly newsletter kept parents informed about the progress and outcomes of the scheme and they were involved with ideas for maintaining interest in the scheme, for example a large 'reminder' poster and 'smiley' badges to encourage users. The scheme was launched with a coffee morning and book sale attended by 15 of the 39 parents.

Over the nine-month period in which the scheme operated, 39 of the 50 children participated and a total of 589 books were borrowed. Approximately 20 books per week were borrowed by the group and borrowing figures for individual children ranged from 1 to 15 books. It is therefore only possible to say that this indicated a good response to the scheme for some children.

The time scale of the Share-a-Book was probably too short to expect any significant changes in the children's literacy development, which was monitored through an observation schedule adapted from Clay's *Concepts about Print Test* (1979). Maturation and literacy support in the homes of these children will have played a large part. Nevertheless, some gains in literacy development were made. An important point was that 23 parents said that the scheme books were shared at home with brothers and sisters, thus benefiting other members of the family. A short questionnaire to parents showed that the scheme had been perceived positively and valued by the parents. Whether it was 'needed' is a contentious issue and raises questions about the nature of such schemes as 'compensatory' or enhancing for all.

The Sheffield Early Literacy Development Project (Weinberger et al., *1990)*

The Sheffield Early Literacy Development Project was a larger scale initiative than those previously described and was supported by a number of grants. The project focused upon working with parents and their children in both their homes and in meetings, in three key aspects of emerging literacy – environmental print, writing and sharing books. The underlying principle of the project is that parents are already playing a key role in supporting and enabling their pre-school children in their literacy development, well before they begin pre-school or primary school. The ideas for involving parents acknowledged this, by building upon the sort of activities which can easily take place in most homes. For example, cutting out pictures and captions from magazines and newspapers and putting them into scrap books.

Home visits centred around a 'Review, Input, Plan' format. 'Review' looked back to the previous visit and asked parents' views on activities which had been suggested or left with them. 'Input' might involve the home visitor using resources for mark making or sharing books. 'Plan' involved talking with the parents about activities which could be left with them and discussing the significance of these for literacy development. Parents were asked to save children's drawings or writing attempts and to date and add comments to these. In the meetings parents were offered information about various aspects of literacy and also shared their ideas and observations (Hannon and Weinberger, 1994). Sometimes parents worked with their own child on literacy-related activities. As one parent said 'We read all sorts now from the top of the bus. We look for words' (p. 11). A project booklet gives guidance for extending this work into other locations such as pre-school groups, schools or libraries. Information from the project has been disseminated in a booklet aimed at parents, pre-school carers and professional educators (Weinberger *et al.*, 1990).

The Learning to Read Programme (Birmingham Community Education)

A key aim of this programme was to demystify the teaching and learning process, to show parents that there is no big secret about it. In commenting upon the programme, Kathy Maclachlan (cited in Strongin Dodds, 1994), who is acting coordinator of Partnership in Education in Strathclyde Regional Council's Department of Education, says that it aims to show parents the 'building blocks' (p. 12) of learning to read. Parents are encouraged simply to talk to their children and to sing nursery rhymes and songs together as an aid to both reading and language development. They are also asked to make up stories based on their own childhood and daily experiences, and to encourage their children to do the same. The parents are advised to have plenty of writing materials such as paper and crayons ready to hand for drawing, scribble and emergent writing. The project is supported by cards containing photographs and suggestions for activities such as Looking at Books and Reading Together which contains suggestions such as 'Look at books together, talk about the pictures. Pictures give clues to words' (Strongin Dodds, 1994).

Shopping to Read Programme (Birmingham Community Education)

The Shopping to Read Programme is another initiative launched by Birmingham Community Education, with sponsorship from a major supermarket. It follows on from the Learning to Read Programme and is based upon the notion that whilst asking a parent to help their child to read may cause anxieties, all parents shop. Shopping trips are utilized through games and worksheets based on making out the shopping list, the shopping trip itself, the return trip and putting the shopping away once home. Inside the shop children are invited to play a variety of games, such as 'I Spy' or identifying labels on tins and packets of familiar items. The project is being developed with parents themselves (Strongin Dodds, 1994).

The ALBSU Project

The Adult Literacy and Basic Skills Unit (ALBSU) Project involves both parents and children in learning together about literacy. The initiative stems from the research findings of the National Child Development Study carried out in the United Kingdom. The research is based on the reading and maths test results of 2,617 children in 1,761 families. Also, on research from the United States, which has demonstrated clear links between parents' difficulties with basic skills and their children's attainment levels in literacy and numeracy. Initial findings from the American family literacy programmes has shown that both adults and children are making positive gains in their learning.

ALBSU are funding a small number of pilot projects. One, based in a low socio-economic area of Bristol involves 30 families who are asked to commit themselves to sessions for 2 to 8 hours a week for 10 to 15 weeks. The project takes place in nursery and primary schools during normal school time. For around half the time the parents work with their children and the other half on their own. One of the two tutors is from the basic education field, the other is a child development specialist (Croall, 1993).

Another ALBSU project based in Norwich, Learning Together, involves parents in a range of activities, for example making a glove puppet as a prop for a story, or learning about different methods of teaching reading. The project is based in a refurbished clinic at a school on a post-war housing estate. On offer are 12-week courses, one-off events and summer activities. Parents are also given a 'tool kit', which is a plastic box with compartments containing crayons, sticky tape, paper and envelopes, so that they can create their own activities with the children. The project aims to reach 150 parents over two years (Spencer, 1994).

The projects: what can be learned?

Attempting to compare projects which employ diverse approaches and operate within different time scales is a difficult task (Bronfenbrenner, 1975). Also, any project will be unique to a particular setting (Parlett and Hamilton, 1977). However, a number of key points emerged which may be helpful to consider when setting up similar projects.

Aims and origins of the projects

The projects derived from different origins which therefore gave rise to different aims; some grew from a need identified in a small-scale setting and were instigated and operated by the people working in that setting. Others were initiated from 'without', in that they have been instigated by those in an advisory, research or support capacity and were therefore targeted at a specific group of children or specific area; for example an educational priority area. The dangers of taking the perspective that groups of children and parents described under the umbrella terms 'disadvantaged' or 'underprivileged' share common characteristics, and that therefore their needs will be met by 'compensatory' input is highlighted by Currie and Bowes (1988). They found this was not the case, as many parents were motivated and were already supporting their children.

An approach which acknowledges and builds upon what parents are already doing may be a better way forward. To quote Kathy Maclachlan again, 'It is not that they lack the initiative, but they are uncertain about the practicalities of teaching their children' (cited in Strongin Dodds, 1994, p. 12). Or, as Chris Dunkley of the Shopping to Read Programme explains:

> We work in areas of need and we help parents to recognize and develop the skills they have. The parents are the children's main teachers and by working in partnership with them we give them the confidence to help and value their children.
>
> (cited in Strongin Dodds, 1994, p. 12)

Resourcing

Finding continuing ways of resourcing such projects is a key issue and appeared not to be resolved for some; funding and book provision was varied. For those projects which were small scale, books and resources from existing classroom or library stock were used. Pulp stock from Penguin Books was obtained by Cooper (1987), who said she 'could worry about maintaining the scheme once it was established!' (p. 101). The larger scale projects were variously funded, some such as The Sheffield Early Literacy Project (Weinberger *et al.*, 1990) and the ALBSU projects through major grants. For those projects not internally resourced, the question has to be raised about what happens when the books or other resources require renewal; this is a central issue for anyone considering taking this step.

Aims and outcomes

A key question was whether the projects achieved their aims, and if so, what could be learned from this. The difficulties of assessing the success or otherwise of projects which do not have comparable information or time scales has already been mentioned. However, the following is an attempt to tease out their success or otherwise. The evaluation of the projects ranged from formal testing and large-scale evaluation to the collection of anecdotal information, often a combination of approaches was used. The smaller scale projects tended to rely upon informal evaluation. A reported high degree of parental interest appeared to be one common strand running through all the projects, although the ways in which this was evaluated varied. Griffiths and Edmonds (1988) reported positive findings from parental interviews and record cards completed by parents. Others monitored this through questionnaires, record cards, attendance at meetings, levels of books borrowed and/or informal comments from parents.

In four projects formal assessment of literacy skills was carried out. Three which used Clay's *Concepts about Print Test* (CAP) or an adapted checklist, showed positive gains in the children's literacy development (Gaines, 1988; Griffiths and Edmonds, 1988; Miller, 1992), whilst the other using an infant reading test did not (Brimer and Raben, 1979, cited in Robson and Whitley, 1989). Whilst direct comparisons of projects are not possible, these four operated for a similar length of time, used a similar book-sharing approach and, apart from the Share-a-Book Scheme, appeared to operate in similar settings. It is therefore possible to speculate that the CAP test is a more sensitive indicator of emergent literacy skills.

Another factor to take into account is that two of the projects which took place in areas designated as social priority areas may have met real needs, thus resulting in gains in development (Gaines, 1988; Griffiths and Edmonds, 1988). To quote Sir Christopher Ball's recent report on the importance of early learning, 'all children benefit, but those whose needs are greatest benefit most' (p. 16). The evidence from the more recent initiatives which have targeted the literacy skills of both parents and children have shown positive gains. In reporting on the ALBSU projects, Croall (1993) quotes Darling, described as a leading figure in the family literacy movement in the United States 'Literacy and the value of education are intergenerational, and the messages transmitted in the home are critical to the future success of the children' (p. 4).

The short time scale of many of the projects increased the difficulties of evaluating what they had achieved. Robson and Whitley (1989) and Miller (1992) suggested this was a possible factor in their projects. One measure of success could be whether the project was to be continued. Some projects were of an exploratory nature which tended to be measured by the high participation rate of the parents within a short time scale (Weinberger, 1988; Cooper, 1987).

Ownership

Ownership of a project is an issue which arose out of my own experience and is not mentioned in other projects reviewed in this chapter (Miller, 1992). In setting up the Share-a-Book Scheme I felt that the playgroup assistants viewed the ownership of the scheme as mine, despite the fact that I was a parent helper and committee member. There had also been a conscious effort to involve the staff in the process of planning and decision making.

This issue of working in partnership in diverse teams is a dilemma which professional educators will recognize, in striving to plan in the context of a team approach. In discussing this, Lally (1991) offers Pugh and De'Ath's (1989) definition of partnership, 'a working relationship that is characterized by a shared sense of purpose, mutual respect and the willingness to negotiate' (p. 33). With the exception of the playgroup leader, who was a trained nursery nurse, it is possible that the sense of purpose was not fully understood in the Share-a-Book Scheme. Another factor may be that involvement in initiatives, such as those described in this chapter, requires a commitment of time and energy which some low-paid, low-status workers may resent giving. Questions must be raised about the quality of provision which relies heavily upon parent help and workers whose training and career opportunities are restricted (DES, 1990). People are more likely to show commitment when they fully participate in planning and decision making. It may be that a project has to arise from a need identified by the workers 'on the ground' in order for ownership to occur.

Partnership with parents

Although the projects reviewed had the common aim of encouraging parental involvement, the notion of partnership seemed to be more fully embraced by some. Cooper (1987), a nursery teacher, talked of meeting parents to establish, 'a scheme that will be acceptable to parents and feasible for me' (p. 102). She confessed to being disappointed by their wish to exchange books at the end of every teaching session, rather than 2–3 times each week as she had hoped; but nevertheless agreed to this. Parents were also adamant that they did not want written instructions, even though as Cooper said, every scheme she had read about seemed to have them.

Such an approach enables parents to make a real contribution to decision making and allows them to share responsibility (Wolfendale, 1985). In contrast, in Currie and Bowes' (1988) project parents were 'interviewed' in order to have the workshops explained to them and the children were at the same time formally assessed. This seemed not to meet Pugh and

De'Ath's definition of partnership previously cited in this chapter (Pugh and De'Ath, 1989, cited in Lally, 1991). Other projects appeared to be at various points along the partnership continuum.

The parents' perspective

The projects reviewed demonstrated parents' willingness to be involved in the development of their young children's literacy skills, yet implicit in some seemed to be a lack of recognition about what parents actually already do with their young children in this key area. In a study which investigated parents' and teachers' perspectives on literacy development in the pre-school years, Hannon and James (1990) found that some headteachers of the schools in which the nursery classes were based, were still expressing doubts about parents' interest in their children. As one headteacher said, 'You won't find much of that in this area' (p. 266). It is, therefore, not surprising that the parents in the study were reluctant to approach the nursery teachers for help. Jo Weinberger (1988) questioned whether parents 'would be interested in being involved' (p. 164) in aspects of their young children's reading development; yet Taylor and Strickland (1986) noted that book sharing was a natural part of family life for the families they studied. Or, as Cooper (1987) says of her project, 'it simply represented an extension of what they were already doing' (p. 102).

A more worrying feature was the parents' concern that what they were doing was not the right thing, to quote Hannon and James (1990), 'You don't want to learn them wrong and then find out when they go to school that they don't know what they're talking about' (p. 265). Cooper says of the parents she worked with, 'Other parents admitted that rather than "do the wrong thing" they had done nothing' (p. 102). Kathy Maclachlan, acting coordinator of Partnership in Education in Strathclyde Regional Council's Department of Education states that 'Many of the parents realize that the only hope for their child is through education, but they are intimidated by the school and the teachers' (cited in Strongin Dodds, 1994, p. 12).

It has been argued that a degree of caution is needed in relation to intervention programmes, which according to Teale (1986) attempt to overlay 'mainstream' or middle-class patterns of interaction on family lives which are not mainstream; or in which the interpretation of terms such as learning, play or reading are not shared (Gregory and Biarnès, 1994). Taylor (1983) goes further and questions the desirability of attempting to change what parents do in the home, referring to what she describes as 'how to' programmes. She argues that changes in home literacy imply changes in the ways in which families organize their everyday activities. This may be particularly pertinent to consider if the culture of the home is 'very distant' from that of the group or school the children enter (Gregory and Biarnès, 1994). This suggests that those programmes which take account of the needs of both parents and children may have more success.

There needs to be a greater awareness among professional educators of parents' contribution to their young children's early education and development. Studies of children in their home settings, particularly in the pre-school years, show that for many children it is uniquely attuned to their needs and capitalizes on 'the stuff of family life' in a way that the pre-school centre or the school cannot (Atkin and Bastiani, 1986, cited in Hannon and James, 1990, p. 270). For other families, who do not share the culture or the values of more formal educational settings, there is a need to develop a shared understanding of what parents and professional educators can achieve together (Strongin Dodds, 1994; Gregory and Biarnès, 1994).

What are required are ways of working with parents which acknowledge that literacy experiences are already part of most young children's lives when they begin pre-school. It therefore follows that professional educators working in pre-school settings will require ways of working with parents which provide a more natural extension between home and school. This review of projects has indicated some ways forward. The final section of this chapter offers a framework to consider which may be helpful when planning for working with parents (adapted from Weinberger, *et al.*, 1990).

A framework for involvement

STARTING OFF

Aims

- What are the aims of the project?
- How will you identify what parents want – questionnaire, a meeting, informal discussion?
- How will you deal with conflicts relating to different ideas about teaching and learning?
- Identify a small number of achievable aims
- Are they feasible?

The target group

- Will the project be aimed at parents, children or both?
- Will it be aimed at all children and all parents?
- If not, what will the criteria for selection be?
- Are parents available?

The setting

- Where will it take place?
- The pre-school group
- The home
- A combination of these
- Other venue

The time scale

- What will be the duration of the project?
- Short term
- Long term
- A pilot project
- Occasional events

GETTING GOING

Communication

- How will parents be contacted – by post, telephone, personal communication, a poster?
- How will you keep them informed – meetings, a newsletter?
- Will there be an information booklet for parents?
- Will there be a home–group or home–school booklet?
- How will changes be negotiated to respond to needs?
- How many different language versions will be needed?

Resources

- Carry out a 'literacy audit' – what is already available?
- Are additional resources needed?
- Is additional funding needed?
- What human resources are needed?
- Are storage facilities sufficient?
- How will the project affect the current setting – space, organization of staffing?

KEEPING GOING

Maintaining impetus

- Reminder posters and leaflets
- Literacy events – book sale, book club, book raffle, book swop, videos about literacy
- Badges for participants

HOW DID IT GO?

Collecting information

- What information will you record in order to know if your aims were achieved – books borrowed, numbers participating, children's learning, whether it was felt to be worthwhile, parental comments?
- How will you record it?

Summary

Children and adults sharing books together is just one feature of the pre-school environment which for many children will enable them to come to know about literacy; book-sharing schemes provide one way of encouraging this activity. Other projects reviewed in this chapter offer a range of approaches to provide links between home and centre-based learning, so that literacy in pre-school centres may bear some resemblance to what has gone before.

CHAPTER 8

Observing and recording early literacy development

Teaching is about moving children on from what they already know and can do.
(Bloom, 1987, p. 30)

In order to move children on from what they already know and can do in relation to literacy development, we need to know where children are in this development. In a recent gathering of people working either with or for young children, Hurst (1994) stressed the importance of professional educators taking account of children's history, which is held by 'historians', i.e. the parents. She spoke about those adults working with young children, 'Catching up on the story which began before you were there'. Catching up on the knowledge and experience which children bring to pre-school settings should be the starting point for assessing their literacy development.

In attempting to find out what young children know about literacy, Nutbrown and Hannon (1993) suggest three aspects of early literacy development which seem worth assessing, these are:

- children's response to environmental print
- sharing books and stories
- early writing.

I would also want to add:

- phonological awareness.

Observing and recording development in these areas in ways which seem appropriate to a range of early years settings is the focus of this chapter.

The assessment of literacy development

Traditionally early literacy development was assessed in relation to readiness for reading, as discussed in Chapter 1, where it was suggested that such tests and profiles do not fit comfortably into an emergent literacy perspective (Harrison and Stroud, 1956; Downing and Thackray, 1972). Methods for assessing early literacy development seem not to have kept pace with the emerging body of knowledge about young children's literacy development (Teale, 1990). In a review of methods of assessment Nutbrown and Hannon (1993) say that though traditional tests have tried to assess children's readiness to acquire literacy, they have not recognized the fact that children are on the road to literacy from a very early age. They acknowledge that this is not surprising, given that emergent literacy is a relatively new framework for understanding the development of young children and many of the tests were developed in the 1960s and 1970s (Goodman, 1984; Teale and Sulzby, 1986). Nutbrown and Hannon (1993) do present the view that valid and reliable formal procedures are needed, in order that teachers and researchers might have measures to evaluate their work in ways which are accepted beyond the classroom walls. However, what is required for professional educators working in a range of early years settings, are more 'naturalistic' means of observing and recording emergent literacy skills (Goodman, 1982; Teale, 1990).

Frameworks for assessing literacy skills

In their book about record keeping in early childhood settings, Bartholomew and Bruce (1993) have noted the need at regular intervals to take stock of where the child is in learning and development, in order to review the needs of the child and the family. They go on to say, 'A number of people have recently been plotting children's progress onto charts with concrete images such as jigsaws, flowers and houses', and continue, 'As well as being user friendly, all of these approaches use aide memoires and prompts rather than checklists' (p. 56). Most of these formats aim to record all the areas of experience which constitute the early years curriculum and not just literacy skills (Ball, 1994). However, some are specifically designed to assess and record literacy development.

Waterland's (1985) reading record takes the form of a wheel with sections covering reading development from pre-school to the end of primary school; but only a limited number of items focus upon emerging literacy skills. These include enjoying books and stories, behaving like a reader, awareness of print. As the child achieves a skill the relevant part of the wheel is coloured in; this provides a record of what the child knows and can do and a basis for future planning. Like Bartholomew and Bruce (1993) I have seen this type of record sheet adapted into a flower, jigsaw or animal format in many primary schools, but for the purpose of recording reading skills.

More recently the Sheffield Early Literacy Development project team (Weinberger *et al.*, 1990) has developed a jigsaw sheet depicting three key aspects of emerging literacy development – sharing books, emergent writing and environmental print. Sections of the jigsaw can be coloured in to record development, for example in relation to developing reading skills: 'tells stories about the pictures'. This provides an easy-to-use format for recording these three key areas of emergent literacy.

In a recent parent workshop based in a nursery school, in which the jigsaw sheets were used, I found that some parents were astonished to see the extent of their child's literacy achievements. Others were surprised that some items constituted important steps towards literacy, for example knowing that books have authors. One parent on completing the jigsaw sheet, talked about the gap in the area of emergent writing skills that she had not been aware of in her child; as she noted, he liked to do other things. The nursery teacher found the information valuable as a basis for discussing the children's needs with the parents and in planning future experiences (Miller, 1991).

The *Primary Language Record* (Barrs *et al.*, 1988) has been designed as a framework for record keeping for children aged 3 to 11, for the purpose of assessing and recording language and literacy skills. It is an observation-based system, involving parents, teachers and children. The format includes keeping diaries of children's language and literacy progress, and discussion sessions with parents and with the children themselves about their achievements. Two teachers, Helen James and Margaret Wyeth (1994) have written about their experiences of using the Primary Language Record. The following is taken from the record of 5-year-old Wing, a bilingual child who speaks Cantonese and English; his 15-year-old sister interpreted for his parents at the 'literacy conference': 'His mum and his sister think that he likes reading a lot. He always likes someone to read to him when he gets home.' The discussion with Wing notes that:

> My favourite thing in school is reading. I like *Cat Sat on the Mat* and *Not Now Bernard.* I can read some books now. I couldn't when I started. My sister teaches me to read. At home I speak Chinese. I get muddled sometimes in English.
>
> (p. 96)

James and Wyeth say that the discussion-based format has led to exchanges of information throughout the school year and have given them a much clearer picture on which to build their planning.

The Early Literacy Project (Andreae *et al.*, 1988) is also aimed, as the title would suggest, at recording early literacy development. The book offers a variety of formats developed by practitioners in nursery and primary schools. The Nursery Monitoring Sheets for Reading and Writing offer a checklist of early literacy skills which provide a framework for observations, plus record sheets for recording this information.

A number of education authorities have devised Early Years Records of Achievement, usually in consultation with practitioners, which tend to take account of 'working towards' the National Curriculum. One example is *Assessment and Record Keeping in the Early Years* (1993a) produced by Manchester City Council Education Department. The Language Record includes writing, handwriting and reading behaviours which include key aspects of emerging literacy development, for example in the Reading Record, 'Joins in and recites from memory – rhymes, stories and refrains.' The language section of Hertfordshire County Council's *Early Years Record of Achievement* (1993) covers similar behaviours and has a section for action and discussion points for parents and other adults to use. Both of these Records of Achievement involve the parents and child at the earliest opportunity.

These or similar frameworks could be used in early years settings as a part of an observation and record keeping system; or, as is often preferred, adapted to suit the needs of a particular group of adults and children.

Learning to see literacy

It was suggested in the previous section that one way of looking at children's emerging literacy development might be through either a published, adapted or individually constructed checklist or observation sheet. The 'Learning to see' of this section's heading is taken from part of the title of a chapter by Drummond (1993) in a book about assessment in the early years; it is preceded by the words 'Looking at Learning'. Learning to see what children know and can do requires skill and knowledge. In choosing a framework through which to observe, 'One is looking through someone else's eyes, and their purposes and perceptions could be very different to one's own' (Hopkins, 1985, p. 10). What Hopkins is suggesting here, is that rather than supporting observations of children's literacy development, such frameworks may constrain and limit what we see. It is possible that observations may focus only upon behaviours and items listed on the checklist, thus other important literacy events may be missed. The best use of these may be as an *aide-mémoire* (Bartholomew and Bruce, 1993) to alert the adult to aspects of behaviour which may be important to record and as a summative record of children's progress and development.

In a summary of what they consider to be the ideal characteristics of useful records for young children, Bartholomew and Bruce include the need to consider a variety of ways in which to assess and record children's development. Many educators of young children are already engaged in using a recording, collecting and dating samples of children's work, taking photographs of work less easily stored, talking to their parents (Nutbrown and Hannon, 1993; Teale, 1990). This assessment process has become more evident and systematic in both primary and many nursery schools and classes since the introduction of the National Curriculum. It is important, however, that there should not be any downward pressure to assess young children because of the National Curriculum; assessment should be for the purpose of getting to know children and what they can do (Bartholomew and Bruce, 1993). At the heart of this process lies the skill of learning to see, of observing children and interpreting what is observed.

Observing literacy development

'All early childhood educators already use observation as an integral part of their daily work' state Drummond and Nutbrown (1992); they go on to say that the implicit, covert skills of observation can be developed and made more explicit 'as we learn to record, examine, reflect and act upon the knowledge we gain through observation and assessment' (p. 97).

The university in which I teach has a nursery school on the premises, Wall Hall Nursery School, which is used in training prospective early years teachers. Each adult working in the nursery has their own notebook to record events and behaviours which seem significant; these are shared with other staff and may later be transferred to a more permanent record sheet. In other pre-school centres I have seen adults involved in recording their observations on to 'post it' notes; these are dated and put into the nursery record keeping book until transferred to a more permanent format. On the teacher training course on which I teach, students carrying out their teaching experience are required to maintain a loose-leaf file with a separate page for observations on each child. Different coloured highlighter pens can be used to highlight important observations relating to a particular area of experience, so that, for example, blue highlights relate to literacy development. The following is an extract taken from the file of a student working in a reception class:

> 20.5. Leslie's drawings are rather scribbly when compared to the rest of the class.
>
> 1.6. During writing news and stories, Leslie gets really agitated and frustrated over his inability to form letters correctly. He needs lots of encouragement so that he doesn't get disheartened.

Such observations would hopefully have led this student to think carefully about the appropriateness of the writing activities which Leslie is being involved in, given the comment about his drawing skills.

Professional educators must 'learn to see' (Drummond, 1993), to observe children in an informed way in order that their assessments are viewed as worthwhile and used by other colleagues, professionals and parents (Teale, 1990; Drummond and Nutbrown, 1992). Observation techniques and assessment and recording frameworks are highly dependent for their credibility upon those who use them. Teale (1990) writes about how the power of informal assessment comes through professional educators being able to see how young children use their emerging skill and knowledge. To quote, 'The great insight for the teacher comes from understanding what the child has done and why the child has done that' (p. 56). In other words, the professional educator needs to learn to see in the professional sense, 'to know what to look for' (Teale, 1990, p. 56).

Observing and recording responses to environmental print

The importance of children's responses to print in the environment was discussed in Chapter 2, as one of the first signs of emerging literacy in young children. As Nutbrown and Hannon (1993) say 'Environmental print is a powerful part of literacy which many teachers know about and incorporate into their teaching' (p. 28). It therefore follows that children's responses and attempts to take meaning from the print they see around them need to be observed and recorded.

Research

There have been attempts by researchers to establish what it is children 'read' in the environment by presenting them with distinctive examples of logos such as McDonalds, both with and without background clues (Hiebert, 1978; Masonheimer *et al.*, 1984). Taking a different approach Kastler (1984, cited in Hall, 1987) presented 5- and 6-year-olds with familiar items such as advertisements, letters and a telephone book, and interviewed them to probe what they understood about the functions and use of the printed material. However, according to Nutbrown and Hannon (1993) there are no published tests to assess this aspect of literacy.

Observation

Information about children's response to print in the environment has also been offered through published accounts of parents' observations of their children (e.g. Lass, 1983; Payton, 1984; Laminack, 1991). Many of these record common occurrences which parents of young children will recognize. The following incident was jotted down as my daughter Katie, then aged 3 years 6 months, was sharing a family lunch on the verandah of a holiday villa. A piece of V shaped spaghetti hung from her fork, 'This is writing' she said. In a later incident she noticed a 'V' shape in the stalk of a flower and asked 'What does that say?' More recently, Katie's 3-year-old cousin Max brought me an 'alphabetti' spaghetti shape saying, 'This is an X'; this letter being significant for Max as it features in his name. Such incidents can provide enormous insights into what children know and the ways in which they attempt to make sense of the print they see around them. In centre-based learning the recording and dating of such incidents can provide a basis for planning appropriate experiences and provide an ongoing record of literacy development.

There is no doubt that young children are very active learners. Harste *et al.* (1984) have written about the way in which children 'test hypotheses' about print in the environment, or in other words, make good guesses about what it might mean. Returning from holiday on an aeroplane Katie noticed some safety instructions on the back of the seats and said, 'Does that say mummy's seat, daddy's seat, girl's seat, lady's seat, man's seat?' As Laminack (1991) has observed, such 'errors' are like microscopes which allow us to see how children are busily constructing meaning from what they see; they use what they know, then try it out. The adult's reaction will then refine and expand the child's knowledge and the child will move forward in development (Vygotsky, 1978). Thus, Katie was using all the available cues around her to try to make sense of the notices in the aeroplane; it was a reasonable assumption that they might be telling people where to sit. Possibly this was based upon past experience of name labels on the playgroup coatpegs or name cards on the table at birthday parties. Further sensitive probing by the adult might reveal more about Katie's reasoning in relation to this incident. Reinforcing her good attempts to work out the labels and giving her the correct information, will take her forward in her development.

In observing his son Zachary's responses to print from birth to 5 years of age, Laminack (1991) suggests that children approach written language from a variety of angles in constructing meaning from print in the environment. They use:

- the general context – logos, the total packaging;
- graphics – size, colour, format, lettering;
- meaning – the object the print occurs on;
- other cues – specific to the individual child.

These observations of Laminack's could offer a starting point for a framework within which children's responses to environmental print could be observed, to establish what it is they are noticing. Observing and recording development in this way provides a window through which to view the child's knowledge and understanding.

Print in the pre-school environment

In order to observe and record children's knowledge of environmental print, it follows that they need to be in a print-rich environment. In the pre-school years this occurs naturally in the home setting or in everyday situations such as shopping at the supermarket or stopping at a STOP sign whilst out in the car. Many household appliances sport the maker's logo, as Laminack (1991) noted, when his young son Zachary read

Figure 8.1 Deepash: Coco Pops

Figure 8.2 Print in the environment

Indesit as 'dishwasher'. An added advantage of the home environment is that it is attuned to the child's cultural background (Gregory and Rashid, 1992–3).

In centre-based learning children need to be provided with opportunities to play and interact with literacy-related objects, in order for those working with them to record what they know and to plan for future development (Hall, 1991). In the Wall Hall Nursery a shop was set up and flooded with familiar packets and boxes such as Kellogs, Frosties, and Crest toothpaste. As the children busily shopped and took packets and boxes in bags and baskets backwards and forwards to the home corner, notes were made by the nursery staff about which aspects of the print the children recognized or responded to.

A book-making activity took place at the same time, in which the children were encouraged to cut out logos from familiar packaging and stick these into their books; many of these were talked about and 'read' back to the parents and staff involved. Figure 8.1 shows Deepash's book cover; he recognized the Coco Pops logo on the packet, cut it out and

Figure 8.3 Print in the environment

copied out the writing. Additional activities provided on the carpet area involved games, simply made from cutting out matching logos from empty packets and mounting these on to card. The children played matching games or 'Snap', as they recognized and 'read' the print.

Environmental print can be incorporated into many aspects of the pre-school centre-based environment. The home corner provides a base for different scenarios; examples I have seen include an estate agents office, a travel agents, a hairdressers salon, a greengrocers shop, an exotic arabian tent, a McDonalds. All these can include posters, packets, notices, newspapers in a variety of languages and other examples of environmental print which can often be freely obtained. The pre-school centre can generate its own environmental print as Figures 8.2 and 8.3 show. Labelling displays and storage facilities provide opportunities to observe whether the children are linking the print with the relevant objects as they take out and replace objects from containers. Changing the birthday chart, finding the correct day of the week or recording how many children are in the class or group that day, allow the adult to observe the children reading and using print.

Planning an environment for literacy in this way, facilitates staff observations and allows for behaviour regarded as significant to be recorded and transferred to a more permanent record keeping system and used as a basis for future planning.

Observing children sharing books and stories

It was established in Chapter 6 that there is powerful evidence that sharing books and stories helps children along the path towards reading. Observing and recording this development will help to monitor children's progress towards conventional reading (Sulzby, 1990). In the Share-a-Book Scheme described in Chapter 7, a means for observing and recording the children's emerging literacy development was needed. Clay's (1979) *Concepts About Print Test* (CAP test) was considered, as it has been shown to have some limited use with pre-school children (Griffiths *et al.*, 1985, cited in Hall, 1987; Clay, 1989; Miller, 1992). The format of the test is a story told aloud from test book, with pictures on one page and the written story on the other. The story is read to the child and the child is asked to 'help' the tester who then asks questions about the book. Test items include book orientation, whether pictures or print carry the message, directionality of writing and pages.

In trying out the test with a group of 3- and 4-year-olds some interesting issues arose relating to testing very young children. My daughter Katie, then aged 3 years 4 months was the youngest child in a group of children 'borrowed' for this purpose. She indicated only the front of the test book and an item showing the direction of the print. It was extremely difficult at times to engage her attention due to distractions such as other children playing outside.

Katie's responses to the test were not at all representative of her considerable emergent literacy skills. Later, whilst sitting in the garden, I engaged her in further conversation about the test book and other books lying nearby. In this situation she was far more responsive and was able to carry out many of the test items which she had previously not responded to. When asked, 'Where are the pictures?', she showed these and talked about them, 'he's on a tree' (the bird) and 'the girl's looking up'. Although in the test situation she did not respond when asked to 'Show me the bottom of the picture'; in the garden with the same item (an upside down picture), she said unprompted, 'It's upside down.' When asked to, she showed the top and bottom of the picture, and when requested to show me a word or letter, she pointed to the print in a general sense. When asked what a page of writing was, 'What are those?' she said 'words'; she then turned the page and said, 'These are words' (Miller, 1992).

It is unlikely that a parent or professional educator would consider using this type of test with very young children. The problem that I shared with other researchers was that I needed a reliable and valid way of assessing the children's literacy skills (Hartley and Quine, 1982). For young children the language and context of test situations can be problematic. Their responses frequently depend upon the questions asked by the adult, therefore, the form of questions used in any assessment situation requires careful consideration if the child is to understand what is required (Donaldson, 1978; Teale, 1990). My particular problem was solved by adapting the CAP test into an observation sheet which could be used in a book-sharing situation (Miller, 1992).

Observing story book reading can provide rich assessment information providing the adult is sensitive to the issues outlined above. Teale (1990) suggests three key contexts in which this can take place:

- one-to-one story book readings;
- adult–child interactions in group settings;
- children's independent emergent story book readings.

One-to-one story book readings

In one-to-one story book readings the child can be closely observed and questions sensitively asked to find out what is known about books and print, and how meaning is extracted from the text. The adult may plan the observation in advance and decide what will be looked for, in which case a framework similar to Clay's (1979) *Concepts about Print Test* could be used. This could include focusing upon whether the child:

- knows which way up to hold the book;
- turns the pages in the right direction;
- shows the pictures;
- shows the writing;
- predicts the story from the pictures;
- tells the story (note use of story language);
- knows where to begin reading the book;
- knows which page to read first;
- joins in and 'reads' a familiar story;
- knows the direction in which the print goes;
- points to the writing as the adult reads;
- notices familiar letters;
- can show a letter/word;
- re-tells a familiar story to the adult;
- shows awareness of letter sound relationships.

In using a checklist-type format as a memory aid, leaving a space for additional comments adds to the assessment. A format such as the jigsaw or similar sheet can be supplemented by written notes. In designing the CAP observation sheet (Miller, 1992) a space was left for additional comments as the following examples show:

Rebecca, aged 4 years 2 months, when invited to look at the pictures in the book and predict what the story might be about said, 'I don't know how to read.'

Jonathan, aged 3 years 4 months, was able to recognize words such as 'look'. In a later observation mentioned in Chapter 6, he showed that he was confident about himself as a potential reader.

Of Daniel, aged 3 years 6 months, it was noted that 'he asked lots of questions about the book' and that 'he "read" the book with great enjoyment'.

Other observations which can be recorded as significant behaviours are noted, as part of daily practice.

Adult–child interactions

Group story book times feature prominently in the daily activities of pre-school centres. It is, however, far more difficult to observe children in a group of between 10 or 20 children than in a one-to-one situation. Also, as Bartholomew and Bruce (1993) point out, current staffing levels in most early years settings rarely allow time for observation and record keeping. Teale (1990) suggests focusing upon one or two children each day, noting factors such as attention, whether the children are able to predict the story appropriately, recalling key parts of the story, their participation in 'reading' along with the text and their comprehension of the story. If another adult can be spared they could sit with the group and take notes.

Some nursery schools and classes who follow a model of curriculum known as 'High Scope' (Langdown, 1989) have small group story times with a key worker, in which case observations may be more manageable. It can also be possible to organize the day so that staff are engaged in sharing stories with three or four children, carrying out observations in this context. Larger versions of popular books or big books, either bought or made, enable the children to see the print and pictures more clearly (Holdaway, 1979).

Children's independent story book readings

Children's independent story book readings provide an opportunity to observe their emergent reading strategies. A comfortable book corner with well-displayed books provides the ideal opportunity. Many young children also enjoy 'reading' stories to dolls and soft toys, so these could be strategically placed in the book corner or home corner, along with a collection of books. Another strategy is to read a story three or four times to a group of children, then ask individual children to 'read' the story back. What they are learning about books and stories can be detected by asking them to 'read' to an adult from a familiar or favourite book (Sulzby, 1986; Teale, 1990). The strategies the child uses to construct meaning from the text can then be observed and noted. These might include:

- labelling and commenting upon the story;
- using the pictures to tell the story;
- synchronizing the story with the pictures;
- use of story language;
- re-telling the story;
- appreciating the sequential nature of the story;
- re-telling a verbatim-like story;
- using expression and elaboration;
- reading independently (Sulzby, 1986; Miller, 1992).

No developmental order is implied in the above strategies, although Sulzby (1986) has found a developmental progression in emergent story readings.

Observing and recording early writing development

In assessing young children's early attempts at writing, the professional educator will be tracing the child's development from emergent to conventional writing. Parents will, of course, be a valuable source of information. The order in which forms of writing may occur, as detailed in Chapter 3, offer a framework within which the professional educator can 'learn to see' children's writing in an informed way. The importance of learning from children's development, in invented spellings for example, and the ways in which letters are formed, provide a basis for the adult to help and support the child towards conventional writing. In a pre-school setting in which emergent writing is provided for and encouraged, children will have ample opportunity to show what they know and can do. Examples of their writing, including those from home, can be retained, dated, commented upon and entered into a portfolio as a record of development.

Significant observations can also be entered into a chosen framework for record keeping, as suggested earlier in this chapter. For example, the Language section of the record booklet produced by Manchester City Council Education Department's *Assessment and Record Keeping in the Early Years* (1993a) offers key statements linked to emerging writing development. Items include 'Enjoys making mark on paper', through to 'Can record simple stories', with a space for dates and comments.

A simplified checklist for use by practitoners for observing early writing behaviour is offered by Sulzby (1990), although she says no order of acquisition is indicated. This covers:

- drawing;
- scribble;
- non-phonetic letter strings;
- invented spelling;
- conventional writing – copying, produced;
- other (to be specified, e.g. abbreviations, calling Braille 'Siamese writing').

In looking at writing development Sulzby (1990) suggests as important noting 'time of onset' (p. 89), that is, noting when a particular form of writing occurs in development. Secondly, to observe the language which accompanies early writing, for example naming letters or reading back what is written, perhaps in the form of 'story language' or a letter to a friend.

The Early Literacy Project (Andreae *et al.*, 1988) materials include a checklist and record sheets for monitoring early writing development, alerting the observer to points to consider, i.e.:

- information about the sample of writing, e.g. where it happened;
- purpose for writing, e.g. name;
- attitudes to writing, e.g. confident;
- script – what the child knows about writing, e.g. scribbling.

In assessing children's writing the tasks we offer to children are crucial, as are the contexts which we provide. Both these aspects are the focus of Chapter 9.

Observing and recording phonological awareness

As noted in Chapter 2, research by Bryant and Bradley (1985) links phonological awareness to later success in reading. Conversely, children who have difficulty in making progress in reading seem to have poor sensitivity to rhyme and alliteration. Bryant and Bradley say:

> Our recommendation then is very simple. Make sure that children have every possible experience with nursery rhymes, and verses and word-games in the years before they go to school. Do everything possible to show them how the words which they speak and hear can be broken up into syllables and small sound segments.
>
> (1985, p. 125)

Drawing upon Chukovsky's work, they suggest that young children's natural enjoyment in playing with words and sounds can be used to advantage.

I am reminded of an incident which occurred on a walk to playgroup with 3½-year-old Katie. I commented upon the door of a house which had been newly painted. Katie immediately responded with 'door, floor'; to which I replied 'tree' and Katie said 'knee'. This game carried on for the one-mile walk, providing a rich opportunity to note her developing awareness of words which sound the same. In pre-school centres similar activities may occur naturally or they can be built into the daily planning.

A student whom I supervised during her nursery-based teaching experience provided an example of planning for phonological awareness. The children, prior to her joining the nursery, had been involved in making a wall display linked to the rhyme, 'Pat-a-cake, pat-a-cake bakers man'; which, after the cake is baked continues 'Pat it and prick it and mark it with B.' They had each baked a dough paste cake in the shape of the initial letter of their first name. These were displayed for the children to see and they were encouraged to find 'their' letter and to see who shared the same letter.

Wishing to build upon this experience, the student initiated a topic on bears. The children brought in their own bears for the display table and made a large bear from a variety of boxes and fabrics; this was mounted on to the display board. The children then painted and cut out, with assistance, several large letter 'b's to surround the bear. Beneath the display was the 'writing table', which featured a letter 'b' mounted in a wooden holder. All this gave the student the opportunity to observe and note down what the children said about the display and whether they could recognize, name and write the letter in this and other contexts. To reinforce this theme, the home corner was turned into the three bears' cottage and a large bear sat in a chair by the message board. Also, many stories and rhymes about bears were read and shared.

An incident in the same nursery shows how informal observations of children's developing awareness of sounds can be noted and subsequently recorded. As a continuation of a 'Festivals' topic, the children were wrapping some nursery toys in christmas paper, so that they could be put around the christmas tree. It was explained to the children involved that the parcels would also be used for a 'guessing game' the next day. Other children would be invited to feel and guess the contents of the parcels. As a visitor to the nursery, I was asked by one child to guess what was inside his parcel; after feeling the shape I asked for a clue. 'It begins with "tr"' he said (it was a train). Thus he showed a good awareness of the 'onset' of the word. This, of course, then escalated into the children giving each other clues about their parcel contents through the initial letter sounds; some more accurately than others!

Children will arrive in pre-school centres with varying amounts of phonological experience. Therefore, the task of the professional educator will be to ensure that each child has a firm grounding in these skills. Experiences with rhyme and alliteration can be carried out as an important part of the daily routine. These will include songs and jingles, tongue twisters, rhyming and word games, and alliteration games such as 'I Spy'

(Goswami, 1994). Practical suggestions are also offered by Meek (1993), i.e. 'Things to Try' (p. 51), so that children who have difficulty can be helped to hear similarities and differences in spoken words, and their progress noted.

Involving parents in assessment

> A crucial point for all infant teachers is to observe each child's responses and attempts at reading and writing in a variety of stimulating activities. Working in partnership with parents will provide further insights.
>
> (Meek, 1993, p. 31)

It has already been seen that parents, albeit in their role as teachers or researchers, can provide a rich source of information about their children (Lass, 1983; Payton, 1984; Laminack, 1991). It therefore makes sense for professional educators to utilize this in finding out about what young children know. Many assessment and record keeping formats described earlier in this chapter recognize the important contribution which parents can and do make, and have been designed to accommodate this.

Cindy Willey, the headteacher of Wall Hall Nursery School, has described the developing knowledge about emerging literacy as 'one of the most exciting developments' in early years education. She has been keen to raise parents' awareness about this development in their own children, through a series of meetings and workshops. I am fortunate to have been involved in some of these sessions. In preparing for one workshop, parents were invited to note their children's responses to print around the home. Figures 8.4 to 8.7 show how sensitive and skilled these parents are in observing their children.

In Figure 8.4 Debbie's mother has provided a wealth of information about her ability to recognize letters and the way in which she uses familiar letters to attempt to read notices in the local environment. Her mother has also recognized that, at the moment, Debbie is recognizing wrappers on the basis of familiar logos rather than the print, although she seems able to 'read' some words such as 'crisps' in the familiar context of the packet. The information recorded by Debbie's mother can be dated and inserted into her portfolio as a record of her emerging literacy development. It can also be added, where relevant, to the nursery records. Pointing out and reading the words is something that Debbie's mother and the nursery staff could focus upon together to take her forward in her development. In this way parents can be fully involved both in assessment and planning for learning.

Lucy's attempts at hypothesis testing (Figure 8.5) have been recorded at home; her term 'Face Meat' is her own construction for naming the contents of the packet. She also has an understanding that the print on the

"Debbie recognises all letters individually, but sometimes gets 'p' and 'q', and 'b' and 'd', confused in lower case.
She often points out words which begin with 'D' for Debbie - this has helped her to recognise the sign in the park saying 'NO DOGS'.
She doesn't show much interest in reading labels on food wrappers, most are recognised but not by the print. I showed her the enclosed packet mostly for the 'ASDA' name which she is always pleased to recognise especially on the big sign outside the store, and she also pointed out the word 'Crisps'."

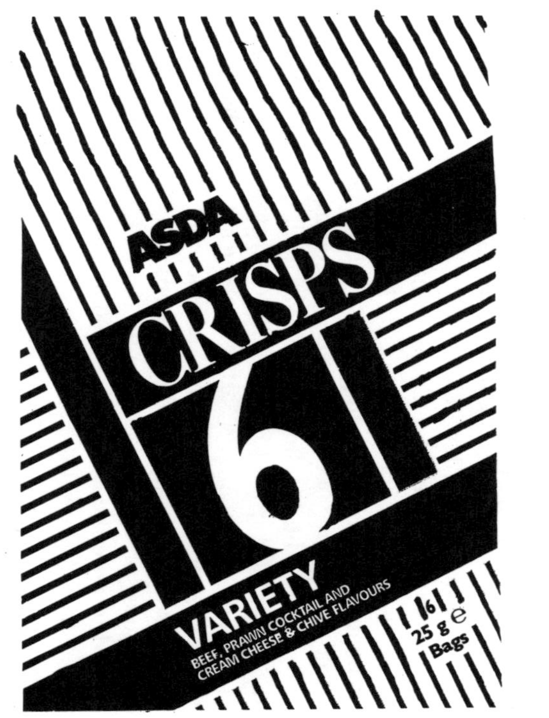

Figure 8.4 *Debbie: Asda Crisps*

Figure 8.5 *Lucy: Face Meat*

Lucy's Comments.

"Picked out 'round' faces with 'round' eyes and triangle 'nose'. Read 'HANSEL & GRETEL' as 'FACE MEAT' as this is her own familiar term for this favourite food.!

Differentiated between all numerals and letters correctly. Named all numbers correctly. Including 6 – (but 'pieces' instead of 'slices'.)

Told me that the meat cost "two, one O, C, T".

Picked out the word 'NO' and read it. Knew no other words.

Named a few of the capital letters – A, S, E, L, F, C.

Namesd most of the lower case letters but found the print very small.

Thought that 'children' said 'Christopher'. (Similar shape word?)

P.S. Enjoyed the guessing aspect of the activity and then insisted on eating most of the contents of the packet!.

"I can read that.

It says 'Happy Shopper'.

I can read something on this packet as well.

(Turns it round and round.)

Ah! There it is.

It says 'Put it in the bin'."

Figure 8.6 Happy Shopper

packet will contain other information such as the price. Additional information can be recorded from this observation by the nursery staff, such as the capital and lower case letters that Lucy is able to recognize. It may be that they could devise activities which would check these out and support this development in other contexts. Figure 8.6 shows a child who is 'behaving like a reader' (Smith, 1985), confidently saying 'I can read that.' A behaviour that nursery staff can build upon by engaging her with print in a variety of contexts. A selection of briefer observations shown in Figure 8.7 further demonstrate how, if given the opportunity, parents can make important contributions to the assessment process. What particularly struck me about these observations was their honesty. At no time have the parents attempted to go beyond the information given, but as with Christopher's mother, they offer an objective assessment. She has recorded that he recognized the letter

Christopher knew the container had vitamins in it. He did not recognise any of the words but he did recognise 'C' for 'Christopher' and also the picture of 'Superted' and told me the vitamins were like teddies and then said they were round! (They are shaped as a teddy).

Christopher knew the bottle contained water. He said he knew it was water because "that's where my drinking comes from " also he said there were waves on the bottle, he did not recognise the word WATER.

Puffed Wheat - "That's got a "p" on it."

Figure 8.7 Puffed Wheat and other observations

'c', no doubt an important letter for him, but made 'good guesses' about the water bottle from the contents and the waves on the bottle. Although these parents took the trouble to record these observations and to bring them into the nursery, less formal links can be made. If alerted to the fact that their children are well on the way to literacy and providing the usual good pre-school contacts have been established, parents can simply be asked from time to time 'What have you noticed?'

The parents in the Share-a-Book Scheme, described in Chapter 7, also demonstrated their skill as excellent observers. Comments in notebooks kept by these parents provided a valuable record of the children's emerging literacy skills and the particular strategies used by individual children, such as pointing to the words or memorizing the story. For example:

10.10.88 Nicholas thoroughly enjoyed this book and memorized it word for word.
9.1.89 Learnt it word for word.
18.1.89 Enjoyed it and memorized short phrases.

16.11.88 Jonathan can pick out words he knows like 'mummy', 'look', 'bird'.
28.11.88 Joined in the words as it was so repetitive.
10.12.88 Read it to himself several times.

3.5.89 Katie moved her finger along the lines and 'read' the last page fairly accurately.

In the Wall Hall Nursery the children take home book bags containing a book of their choice as well as home–school notebooks, in which parents can comment. These form the basis for further discussion with parents and contribute to records of literacy development. Parents are also involved in contributing information to the nursery checklist of development through discussion at parent evenings and through home visits.

Summary

The skills involved in observing and recording early literacy development require those working with young children to receive high-quality training. This should include an up-to-date knowledge of emerging literacy development. Whilst acknowledging that adults working with the under fives will be differently qualified and will have different backgrounds and experience, the Rumbold report *Starting with Quality* (DES, 1990) gives a detailed list of the knowledge, understanding, skills and attitudes which adults working with the under fives need to possess. Some of these seem particularly relevant to this chapter. These are:

- understanding of the way children learn;
- knowledge of recent research and understanding of its implications in relation to the provision of quality experiences for young children;
- observational skills and effective recording, monitoring and assessment of the curriculum.

CHAPTER 9

Provision for literacy in the pre-school

The previous chapter stressed the importance of professional educators observing and recording children's responses to literacy, in partnership with parents where possible. To return to the garden analogy in Chapter 1, in order for the roots of literacy to grow, they need an environment in which they can be nurtured. For many children such an environment will have been provided in and around the home setting. When moving to centre-based learning, children need to find themselves in settings which reflect what has gone before, in terms of the child's culture and previous experiences, and in which literacy skills and knowledge can be displayed. Unless centre-based learning in the pre-school years provides this continuity, then considerable time, knowledge and energy will be wasted.

Environments for literacy

In describing good practice in the early years in language and literacy provision, HMI (1989) identifies two key features, these are well-planned provision and adult interaction. In a wider consideration of high-quality early education, the *Start Right* report (Ball, 1994) says three main factors are implicated, the physical setting, the curriculum and the quality of the adults. Chapters 9 and 10 provide a consideration of these key factors in relation to provision for literacy.

Literacy in the curriculum

Language and Literacy is one of the key areas of experience in the early years curriculum (HMI, 1989; Langdown, 1989). English is a core subject in the National Curriculum and includes speaking and listening, reading and writing. It is important, however, to hold on to the principles which underlie curriculum planning in the early years, that is, that for young children learning is holistic and not separated into subject groupings (Early Years Curriculum Group, 1989; 1992). To cite the Early Years Curriculum Group (1992), 'Young children learn about "subjects" through a variety of play activities' (p. 19). In describing good practice and effective teaching in language and literacy provision in the early years, HMI (1989) describes environments in which teachers and other adults (including parents) interact with books and other types of printed material, and where books can be taken home to share with parents. Imaginative play contexts, such as a hairdressers, give rise to functional writing skills. Suggestions for providing similar contexts and activities based upon play and learning through first-hand experience, but relating to planning within the National Curriculum, are to be found in The Early Years Curriculum Group publication (1989) and in Manchester City Council Education Department (1993b) *English in the National Curriculum: Key Stage One Resource Pack.*

In the pre-school years literacy will take place across 'subjects' or areas of experience. For example, in their nursery, Edward and Anna had painted caterpillars which they had observed. They then dictated to the adult what they wanted to 'say' about their paintings and this was written down for them. Anna dictated, 'A wiggley caterpillar, a straight caterpillar and one curled up.' Edward said 'My caterpillar's on top of the leaf.' Because it is their own speech written down, they are able to read it back, thus behaving like conventional readers. So, literacy may occur in the context of a scientific exploration, where drawings and models of living things are made and written about, and reference books consulted with the help of the adult (HMI, 1989). As was stressed earlier in this book, any compartmentalizing of 'subjects' and their divisions, for example, reading and writing, are made for ease of writing about the various aspects of literacy development; it is acknowledged that they are integrally tied (Sulzby, 1990). Therefore, in the pre-school years the literacy curriculum will be firmly embedded in holistic functional contexts which reflect real life experiences.

The physical setting

In the pre-school years most home settings will provide a rich natural context in which events, such as shopping, cooking, writing out party invitations, give rise to opportunities for literacy. In centre-based learning such opportunities will need to be planned; play will provide the natural context for the planning of literacy experiences (Hall, 1991; Neuman and Roskos, 1991; Mandel-Morrow and Rand, 1991). Nigel Hall (1991) compares the risk taking which young children can safely engage in, in a play context, to the 'have a go' strategies which they use in working out and trying out the functions of print. Laminack (1991) describes this as 'trying it on for size' (p. 83). Indeed, early attempts at reading and writing are often described as 'play writing' or 'pretend reading'. 'Oral storying' in imaginative or 'socio-dramatic' play allows children to rehearse stories they have heard (Fox, 1992). General links have been made with this ability and later story writing (Hall, 1991, citing Wolf and Pusch, 1985).

Providing literacy-related resources is an obvious step towards encouraging children to act in literate ways. In specifically enhancing literacy-based play opportunities in two pre-school classrooms, Neuman and Roskos (1991) found an increase in the children's literacy play and literacy development. In a review of studies involving changes in the physical environment in a range of early years settings, in order to promote literacy development, Mandel-Morrow and Rand (1991) found increases in the voluntary literacy behaviours of children during play. As Hall (1991) says, 'Play provides a context within which the emergence of literacy can be manifested and explored' (p. 20).

A literacy audit

In planning for a literacy-enriched play environment, a useful starting point is to carry out a 'Literacy Audit'. This can be done under the following headings:

Planning the environment

The settings in pre-school centres are often arranged into different areas related to different activities. In analysing existing provision for literacy, it may be helpful to sketch a scale plan of the room and place paper or card templates of all the movable items in the room, such as cupboards, tables, book cases, on to the plan. These can then be moved around to create more clearly defined areas to encourage literacy play; for example a book area, a writing area, an office centre, a kitchen area, a hairdressers, the home corner. This may be particularly helpful in playgroup settings where equipment often has to be stored away after each session. These areas can of course be planned flexibly and changed to reflect current curriculum themes, maybe around topics of interest and the children's changing interests.

No doubt considerable literacy opportunities will already be present in most pre-school settings, but carrying out this activity in the context of team planning, allows for a fresh look at provision and will hopefully generate new ideas. In undertaking a similar activity, Neuman and Roskos (1991) found it helpful to site 'literacy-enriched centres' apart from noisier areas such as the Block Play area. They also found that locating certain areas adjacent to each other encouraged the development of sustained play themes, for example going from the post office to the library. Having considered the potential of the physical environment in supporting and fostering literacy-related activities, these areas will then need to be resourced.

Resources for literacy

Resources or 'props' for literacy will be determined by the nature of the area into which they are put, although some, such as writing implements and materials will have more general application. Neuman and Roskos (1991) have developed the following criteria which may be helpful in choosing and collecting resources:

- *Appropriateness:* can the prop be used safely and naturally by young children? (Some of Neuman and Roskos's concerns, for example about the safety of staplers and paper clips seem a little surprising, as I have seen these widely used by young children even without close supervision).
- *Authenticity:* is it a 'real' item? For example, business forms, cookery books, coupons and telephone note pads rather than the home-made version. As Neuman and Roskos (1991) note, many children will be familiar with such items and therefore could rely on previous knowledge and experience to extend their play.
- *Utility:* does the prop serve a particular function that children may be familiar with in their everyday life? For example, props associated with posting a letter, i.e. envelopes, (used) stamps, writing implements. Does it relate to the purpose of the area? For example, a pad for writing down food orders in the cafe.

'Brainstorming' the props required when setting up a particular area can give rise to extensive lists. This can include an 'audit' of existing resources and a basis for adding to these where needed. The following is adapted from one of four lists generated by Neuman and Roskos (1991, p. 175):

Kitchen

- books to read/dolls/animals
- telephone books
- a real telephone
- emergency numbers list
- cookery books
- blank recipe cards

- labelled recipe boxes
- fridge magnets with print logos
- a message board
- food coupons
- grocery ads/fliers
- money
- empty food containers and packets, cleaning materials, etc.
- calendars
- pens, pencils, markers
- carrier bags with writing and logos
- large plastic clips
- food posters

Storing resources on a thematic basis, e.g. in large plastic containers, labelled 'Cafe', 'Hairdressers', aids future planning; although of course some props, such as telephones, telephone directories and message pads will serve more than one area.

Print in the environment

The importance of planning a print-rich environment within which children's responses to print can be observed, was stressed in the previous chapter. Once again, carrying out an 'audit' of the print in the pre-school setting can help to focus upon opportunities for further development.

- How much print is there in the room?
- Does it vary in type?
- Is it at the children's eye level?
- Can use be made of hanging mobile labels?
- How much environmental print is there?
- Are boxes, drawers, storage containers labelled? (Pictures, photographs or real objects, e.g. pencil to indicate contents provide further support.)
- Are key areas labelled, e.g. The Writing Area? (Adapted from Neuman and Roskos, 1991.)

Figures 8.2 and 8.3 show a range of print photographed in a reception class. Through the labelling of key areas and storage areas children are enabled to understand the *function* of print, for example, that this is where the pencils are stored. They can also see the *form* of print, i.e. the word 'pencil'. In one early years classroom an environmental topic on litter gave rise to a display featuring print in the environment. The children made posters using a range of cut-out letters from magazines and catalogues, featuring messages such as 'Don't Drop Litter'. The poster display was surrounded by a variety of 'litter' which the children had collected, including crisp bags and chocolate wrappers; all featuring a range of logos to be read.

Meek (1993), in a discussion of young children's need to learn the relationship between the sounds and the letters of the alphabet, suggests there are advantages in 'starting off' with capital letters; she links this to environmental print. Meek argues that most print, labels and signs in the environment are in capital letters. Certainly the examples in Figures 8.1, 8.4, 8.5 and 8.6 show this to be the case. Also, that capital letters are more distinctive from each other than lower case. She cites case studies of 'precocious' readers (p. 51) who have shown a preference for using capital letters. More anecdotally, my own observations show that many young children use capital letters in their emergent writing. This is something that traditionally many professional educators believe children have to 'unlearn' and often ask parents to discourage this.

Creating scenarios for literacy play

Once a literacy audit has been carried out, planning or revising existing literacy provision can begin. Most pre-school centres, including reception classes, will have the equivalent of a home corner or play house. Such an area can easily be flooded with print. For example, a telephone directory and message pad by the telephone, milkman/woman messages, newspaper, catalogues, holiday brochures, old cheque books, pool coupons, magazines, circulars and blank forms to fill in, wall posters, writing paper and envelopes. The kitchen area can be supplied with various food packets, a message board (the wipe clean variety are fun, but the writing is then 'lost'), carrier bags with supermarket logos, cookery books and recipe cards. Picture and story books will feature, as will dolls and soft toys to read them to. The print will of course, as far as possible, reflect the language and culture of the children in the centre.

Hall (1991) describes how, with colleagues, he adapted the home corner in a nursery classroom and set up a play situation in which literacy was 'an embedded feature'. The area was subjected to a 'print flood', which included equipment for an office area. During four days of observation 290 events exhibiting literacy-related behaviour were observed. The children demonstrated their knowledge of the purposes of print and also an understanding of the social context in which print is used. They also engaged in a wide range of mark making.

Although the home corner provides an ideal setting for different scenarios, these can also be created in other areas of the room. The following are examples of some successful settings which I have observed in preschool centres.

The estate agents

A wooden framework which had previously served as a shop was converted into an estate agents. The nursery children had been engaged in a topic on 'Homes'. They had looked at houses in the local area and taken photographs of these, noting name plates on roads and the numbers of houses. These were made into an adjacent display and the children's drawings and emergent writing were put into a house-shaped book. Books featuring house and home themes, including reference books, were also prominently displayed to encourage the children to use them. The children had been taken in small groups to visit a local estate agent and had returned with a range of printed materials such as house details, posters and business forms. The children drew and wrote their own house details and made FOR SALE and SOLD notices. Alongside was a carpeted area for block play where, continuing the homes theme in a historical context, a castle had been built by the children.

The cafe

The home corner in a nursery class provided the basis for the cafe setting, but this was continued into an adjacent outside covered play area. Tables were set with cloths and small pots of flowers. Sandwiches were made and labelled. Cakes were baked, which of course involved consulting recipe books. Menus were written, orders noted and bills made out; telephone bookings were taken. Posters advertising special dishes of the day adorned the walls. Considerable language was generated associated with cafes and food and opportunities for role play.

To list all the possible scenarios through which literacy play might be generated could probably fill a chapter of this book. Helpful suggestions have been listed elsewhere (The Early Years Curriculum Group, 1989; Campbell, 1992; Manchester City Council Education Department, 1993). However, some particularly interesting ones which I have seen are: Toys' Я' Us; Pizza Hut; a hat shop; and a garden centre (which generated the seed packets shown in Figures 3.5 and 3.6).

In planning for literacy play, Hall (1991) cautions against 'making play an instructional context for literacy' (p. 21). Tina Bruce (1991) also warns against heavily pre-structuring play, 'Certainly adults can "offer" materials, stories and themes, but it is for the children to "own" them, or indeed be allowed not to take up the offers' (p. 25). In the pre-school years the task of the professional educator is to provide a context in which literacy-related resources can be explored, without pressure to produce an end product.

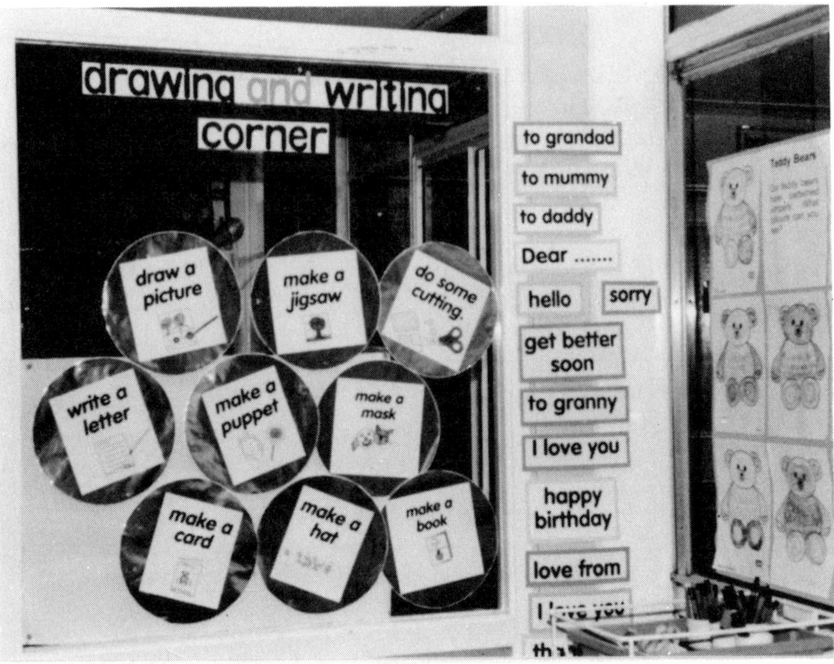

Figure 9.1 A writing area

The writing area

A writing area is an area designed to encourage children's emergent or independent writing. An area such as the one shown in Figure 9.1 is easily created with the use of existing tables and storage trays. Writing areas which I have seen in a range of early years settings have notices which invite the children to write. Key words and the letters of the alphabet are displayed so that the children may choose to use these in their independent writing attempts. A message board provides a purpose for sending and receiving written communications. Resources for writing can be stored in labelled boxes, containers and baskets to encourage the children to tidy them away after use; this also provides opportunities for the children to 'read' the labels. Pictures or photographs of the objects placed alongside the print provide a further aid to learning. Manchester City Council Education Department's publication, *English in the National Curriculum: Key Stage One Resource Pack* (1993b, p. 91) provides an extensive list of resources which could be put into a writing area. These are listed below but with some additions:

- pencils (various)
- felt tips (various)
- biros
- wax crayons
- pencil crayons
- chalks
- pastels
- variety of paper in different sizes, shapes, colours
- envelopes
- postcards
- ready-made books
- used greetings cards
- chalkboard
- message board
- letter stamps
- dictionaries
- post box
- stapler and staples
- ruler
- sellotape
- underlays covered in clear plastic
- pencil sharpener
- paper clips
- hole puncher
- soft or hard plastic, wooden or felt letters
- magnetic letter board and letters
- felt letter board
- typewriter
- concept keyboard and printer.

Not all these resources would be put out at once, but varied to maintain interest or to facilitate particular skills. One of the most important ingredients is, of course, an adult to sit down and write alongside the children (Campbell, 1994). In many visits to pre-school settings I have found this always attracts the children to the writing area. The importance of the adult in providing a model for both reading and writing has been emphasized in previous chapters.

The library area

Children sharing books with adults is an important part of early literacy development as discussed in Chapter 6. It therefore follows that this opportunity should be a key feature of any pre-school centre. Almost all will have a library area or book corner; however, these may vary greatly in terms of the quality of books available and the attractiveness of the setting. Suggestions for 'ideal areas' (Mandel-Morrow, 1991; Campbell, 1992; Manchester City Council Education Department, 1993b) include:

- preferably a quiet location
- a screened-off area – to give an atmosphere of privacy
- book shelves for general storage with the book spines showing
- open-faced shelves to display the covers or inside pages
- storage baskets or boxes
- a rug or carpet, pillows, bean bags, floor cushions, small sofa
- a story board
- a listening corner with tape recorder and headphones
- attractive posters
- stuffed animals and dolls
- magazines and newspapers
- small tables
- a display space for related children's work.

Because of financial constraints, adults working in pre-school centres are ingenious and resourceful, and are able to create stimulating environments with limited resources. For example, in a playgroup in which I worked an attractive book corner was created using wooden screens, open storage shelves, a rug and floor cushions made or donated by parents and brightly coloured bean bags paid for by fundraising activities. A good range of books were borrowed from the library service and others bought with the proceeds of book sales.

In an open plan nursery school where a quiet space was hard to find, a listening corner was created in the headteacher's office. There were two tape recorders and headsets and a collection of books with accompanying felt finger puppets representing the characters in the books. The Ahlbergs' (1977) book about Burglar Bill, Burglar Betty and the baby was a particular favourite. 'Listening packs' comprising finger puppets made by a parent, the book and tape were stored in labelled shoe boxes. Figure 9.2 shows equipment for listening to taped stories located in the book corner in a reception class. A cosy and private listening corner was created by a student undertaking a teaching experience in a nursery class. Lengths of fabric were hung from floor to ceiling in a corner of the room to form an enclosed area. A rug and large floor cushions were provided, so that the children could look at books and listen in comfort to the many tape recorded stories. An extensive list of story tapes suitable for the early years can be obtained from Madeleine Lindley Ltd.

Figure 9.2 *A listening corner*

Choosing books for children

If it is established that books are an important part of overall literacy provision for young children, then the question follows as to whether the choice of books matters. It seems that it does. The studies referred to in Chapter 6, suggest that child–adult interactions with books, and children's subsequent literacy development are affected by the types of book chosen. It therefore seems important to give some attention to criteria to consider when selecting good quality books for the book area. However, as Nutbrown (1994) says, 'It is all very well to talk of "quality books", but not so easy to define what quality consists of' (p. 94).

I found that parents keeping 'book-sharing notebooks' (Miller, 1992) demonstrated clear ideas about what constituted a good read with their children. The importance of tension and climax were mentioned:

> The successive anti-climaxes heightened the tension and helped to keep Catherine's attention through to the end of an otherwise very long children's story.

Good illustrations were seen as important:

> . . . asked lots of questions about the story and the pictures.
>
> . . . could tell the story from the pictures.
>
> Nice colourful pictures.
>
> The illustrations were very good.

However, as Nutbrown (1994) notes, quality is a very personal construct and when applied to choosing books individual taste will play a major role. Catherine's mother shows this:

> Catherine enjoyed the basic story. Having read it to her once I returned it as I didn't like the ending about being dead. Death in any form is unnecessary at this age in stories.

It is therefore more fruitful for early years workers to develop their own criteria for choosing books for children (Nutbrown, 1994). However, some helpful criteria to consider when selecting books for children is offered by Nutbrown. This has been developed by Madeleine Lindley of Madeleine Lindley Ltd, based on work carried out during Manchester's Early Literacy Project (1984–8). I am grateful to Madeleine Lindley for her permission to reproduce this criteria here, in the format agreed by her with Nutbrown:

Appeal
- Does the book look inviting?
- Consider size, colour, illustration, title.

Readability
- Does the book's form/structure make reading easy?
- Do illustrations complement the text?
- Is the story line predictable, making sense to children and thus encouraging reading for meaning?
- Does the language flow naturally, not sounding stilted or contrived? How close is it to children's own speech patterns (important at early stages)?
- Is the print helpful and appropriate for reading level? Look at size of type, position on page, amount on page, line endings.
- Consider the length of the book.

Content
- Is the content worth reading?
- Does the story hold the reader's attention with characterization or plot?
- Does it extend the child's imagination and emotional range *or* relate to the children's own lives, experiences and feelings?
- Do you enjoy it yourself? (But remember that tastes vary.)

- Does non-fiction present information in an interesting and accessible manner, appropriate to the age of the reader but without trivializing the subject?

Development

- Will this book help the child to develop into a more skilled reader?
- Does it enrich the child's vocabulary and an understanding of different language uses (e.g literary language)?
- Does it enable use of a variety of reading strategies depending on purpose?
- Does it raise questions and encourage development?
- Does it stimulate a creative or imaginative response?

Equal opportunities

- Is the writer conscious of equal opportunities and attempting to avoid bias?
- Consider the implicit message of the book as well as the detail.
- Are there positive views of minority-group people and reference to their cultural traditions, where appropriate?
- Are female characters given equal importance and status as males?
- Are stereotypes avoided and are images of ethnic origin, religion, class or disability fairly and positively shown?

Considering these criteria as a staff group in the context of existing library stock, and when choosing new books, could prove a useful and worthwhile exercise.

Waterland (1985) also offers guidance to 'worthwhile texts', which includes qualities to be found in Lindley's list, e.g. reading aloud well, having natural language rhythms, a close match between the text and illustrations, humour, tension and pattern. Familiarity is seen as a valuable attribute.

In selecting books as part of literacy provision, thought also needs to be given to the range and variety to be made available.

Picture books

Pictures play an important part in book sharing in the earliest years, providing a framework for naming objects and characters and a focus for children's questions. As children become familiar with their favourite stories, the text then becomes increasingly important. A close match between illustration and text provide an important aid to meaning, as pictures provide non-verbal representations of ideas. Children can be invited to predict, remember and use story language to 'tell' the story from the picture (Bennet, 1985).

Rhyme

Rhymes, a key feature of many pre-school settings, are known to play a role in later success in reading (Bryant and Bradley, 1985; Goswami, 1994). Rhymes play an important role in developing children's awareness of the sounds which make up words. Participation through movement involving action rhymes, can strengthen a child's understanding. Single nursery rhymes presented as a book can help the child who knows the words to behave like a reader, until there is a match between what is said and the words on the page (Bennet, 1985). Meek (1982) has said, 'If you want your child to read early, link your saying and singing of nursery rhymes to their presentations in books specially prepared for children' (p. 34). Big book versions of nursery rhymes are now available. It is therefore important to include nursery rhymes and poetry books when offering books to young children.

Novelty books

There are many books available which contain novelty features such as pictures and messages hidden behind flaps or in pockets such as *The Jolly Postman* by the Ahlbergs (1986) or those with sounds, music or 'scratch and sniff' properties. The following notes made by Adam's mother in their book-sharing notebook about Eric Carle's (1970) book *The Very Hungry Caterpillar* illustrates this, 'Always a favourite. Counts the fruit. Names everything he eats on Saturday. Puts his fingers in the holes. In fact knows it virtually off by heart' (Miller, 1992). Such books entice children to explore their contents and request, as Adam did, repeated readings, leading to attempts to 'read' independently. However, caution is needed if they distract from an otherwise dull and uneventful text, accompanied by an interesting story line they can be a bonus (Pearson, 1990).

Comics and comic features

Comics and comic features, such as a 'balloon dialogue', can have a role to play in that picture and text are closely linked and have to be interpreted together. However, sometimes parents are uncertain about their value. In my own study (Miller, 1992), one parent said comics were 'not allowed', although over the project period they grew in popularity with the children. Meek (1988) suggests parental uncertainty about their value may add to their appeal!

Workbooks

This type of book is unlikely to be found in the book area, but such books do find their way into children's homes and sometimes into pre-school centres. A narrow concentration on 'workbooks', emphasizing the alphabet, numbers, shape, colour – leading into 'workbook' activities, seem to have a negative effect on later school achievement (Heath, 1982). This may be because opportunities for cooperative book sharing are reduced, for example the adult asking 'open-ended' questions such as 'What might happen next . . . ? What if . . . ?' or linking the content to the child's experiences and expanding general knowledge; thus the book affects the nature of the interactions (Tizard and Hughes, 1984). There are far more interesting ways of presenting literacy to children.

Big books

Large versions of books enable the adult to share a book more easily and more intimately with a group of children, thus simulating book sharings with parents and providing an extension to home experiences. Popular stories can be enlarged and perhaps illustrated by the children; however, commercial copies are available. An excellent book list, *Big Books for Literacy Development* is available from Madeleine Lindley Ltd, containing both traditional tales and contemporary stories; many with accompanying cassette tapes. Smaller versions of big books can be taken home to share with parents. It seems worth quoting the following justification for using big books:

> Enlarged texts, home made or carefully selected for quality, are useful for groups. The teacher will demonstrate and develop with pupils the various strategies for making sense of print. At Level 1 these will include using illustration, rhyme, rhythm and memory to predict the text. Other pupils will be ready to pay attention, within a familiar text, to picture and context cues, identifying known words, using phonic knowledge and considering punctuation.
>
> (Manchester City Council Education Department, 1993b, p. 72)

Although referring to children following Key Stage 1 Programmes of Study within the National Curriculum, all of this can apply to children in the pre-school. Additionally the adult can model other aspects of the book-sharing situation, for example turning the pages, pointing out author and title or showing the direction of the text by finger pointing. Focusing upon particular letters and drawing attention to alliterative sentences will help to develop phonemic awareness. Big books also allow for two or more children to comfortably share a book together, perhaps whilst listening to an accompanying story tape. Holdaway (1979) offers detailed descriptions of the use of enlarged books in early years settings.

Reference books

Simple well-illustrated reference books can be introduced to young children. The adult can share these individually or in small group situations. The contents can be discussed, and Contents and Index pages can be pointed out. Reference books linked to current topics may be displayed on an interest table. Figure 9.3 shows a display relating to mini-beasts in a reception class. Nearby was a related display linked to the topic of 'Growth'.

Figure 9.3 Reference books

The children had produced a 'Growing Diary', which was a home-made reference book containing the children's recordings and drawings of the growth of some beans.

Fairy tales

A criticism of 'stripped down' versions of traditional stories is made by Wolf and Heath (1992) which they believe can divest stories of emotional impact and rich language. They suggest many simplified children's books 'invite no concern with abstractions such as beauty, love, intention, loyalty, faith and persistence' (p. 190). Original versions of, for example, Grimm's Fairy Tales were read to the two young children in their study. Such stories can be read to young children with appropriate gestures and props.

Story readings in the pre-school

Traditionally, story reading in groups involves the adult reading to a large group of children. This is a very different experience to the intimate, interactive story readings which hopefully many children will have experienced at home. This difference is often evidenced by their inclination to gaze around the room, play with any object near to hand, or as in some instances, to escape the situation! Children will arrive in pre-school centres having experienced literacy in very different ways. Some children may need to learn what a book is, and that it is handled differently to other objects. Others may be ready for discussions about familiar stories and may wish to 'read' to the adult. Whilst recognizing the difficulties of implementing a small group or individual story reading in groups of 25 to 30 children, it may be that some thought could be given to alternative arrangements, at least on some occasions and especially for those children most in need, who do not have a history of being read to. The services of parents or volunteers and older children have all been used with some success. Many pre-school centres invite parents to share books with their children at varying times throughout each week. Careful choice of books and plentiful opportunities for sharing them are therefore an important part of the planned experiences of every pre-school centre.

Summary

The thrust of this chapter has been that literacy in the pre-school years must be embedded in contextualized experiences; that is, experiences which are as far as possible linked to functional real life contexts which build upon what the child has engaged with before. There will be children in pre-school centres who require literacy experiences not yet encountered, others will be more ready to take advantage of what is offered. Therefore, literacy in the pre-school will be part of the continuum of the child's emergent literacy development, and so must parallel and complement what happens in the home, in order that the child can feel comfortable in the setting provided. Whilst acknowledging that the role of the pre-school is different to that of the home, some continuity of experience is crucial if it is to build upon what has gone before.

CHAPTER 10

The supporting adult

> The role of the adults is crucial in facilitating the experiences that the children have with literacy.
>
> (Campbell, 1992, p. 3)

The previous chapter emphasized the role of the professional educator in planning and providing for rich literacy experiences in pre-school settings, in order that young children may have the opportunity to demonstrate what they know and can do; but, of course, this is not enough. The quality of those adults and adult interaction have been identified as crucial factors in providing high quality early years education (HMI, 1989; DES, 1990; Ball, 1994). In Chapter 8 it was suggested that the knowledge, skills, understanding and attitudes of adults working with young children would considerably influence their capacity to observe, record and respond to children's literacy development with an informed eye. It was argued that they must 'learn to see' literacy development in such a way that they are able to support young children and take them forward in that development.

The role of the adult in emergent literacy

The professional educators' view of literacy will considerably influence the way in which literacy is presented in the pre-school setting. If literacy is seen as part of a continuum of emerging skills which begin to develop in the first months of life, then the role of the adult in the pre-school will be to establish where each child is along that continuum, and to help the child on from there. This is best done in collaboration with parents. In this case literacy will build upon what has gone before, even if previous experience has been sparse or culturally different. If, however, literacy is viewed as beginning when the child enters the more formal educational setting, and parents are not involved in establishing where the child is, then literacy will be a different sort of experience.

This difference is illustrated by Harste *et al.*'s (1984) account of 6-year-old Alison on beginning 'first grade'. Alison entered her first-grade class as a confident emergent reader and writer; delightful examples of her writing show her considerable knowledge of the system. Her teacher, however, did not provide Alison with the opportunity to demonstrate what she knew. In school Alison was required to write underneath the teacher's writing. On returning home with this 'work' Alison's father asked her to write out the same sentence, 'Here is my home and family', which she wrote as 'HOROS MI HOS ADND FAMILE'. Alison then promptly burst into tears saying 'I can't write', and even after reassurances that she could, and had been writing for a long time, she said, 'But I don't know how to spell and write good' (p. 14). The point Harste *et al.* wish to make is that adults need to take risks in order to challenge long-held assumptions about what literacy looks like in pre-school settings and early years classrooms. They argue that this teacher was constrained by her assumptions about literacy and was therefore unable to allow Alison to demonstrate what she knew about reading and writing.

Four-year-old Max appears to be similarly constrained in his day nursery, albeit unconsciously, by the adult concerned. Writing down what Max has to say, as in Figure 10.1, is a reasonable supportive strategy. It enables him to see that what he says can be written down and read back, it also frees him from the constraints of writing this for himself. However, knowing that they then have to 'write good', to use Alison's term, what they have dictated, will often hold children back from their oral storying. There is also the danger that children will imbibe the message that their own writing does not count, that 'conventional' writing involving forming letters correctly and memorizing words is the only writing which is valued. Sulzby (1990) has written about this approach, known as the 'Language Experience' approach, saying that although it shows that the child's oral language and emergent reading is valued, a different message is conveyed relating to the form of writing. Sulzby suggests a way forward may be to use a strategy which I have observed in a number of pre-school centres and early years classrooms, which is for the adult to distinguish between 'grown-up' or 'teacher's writing' and 'children's writing'; so that, to use Sulzby's words, children write for themselves in their own way alongside the adult's writing. Using this approach would have allowed Max and Alison to show what they know about the writing system and therefore a rich opportunity for assessment would not have been missed.

Similar constraints can operate in relation to emergent reading. I have previously written about the following incident, 'Katie, aged 5 years, whilst playing at home, was asked if she would like to get a book that we could

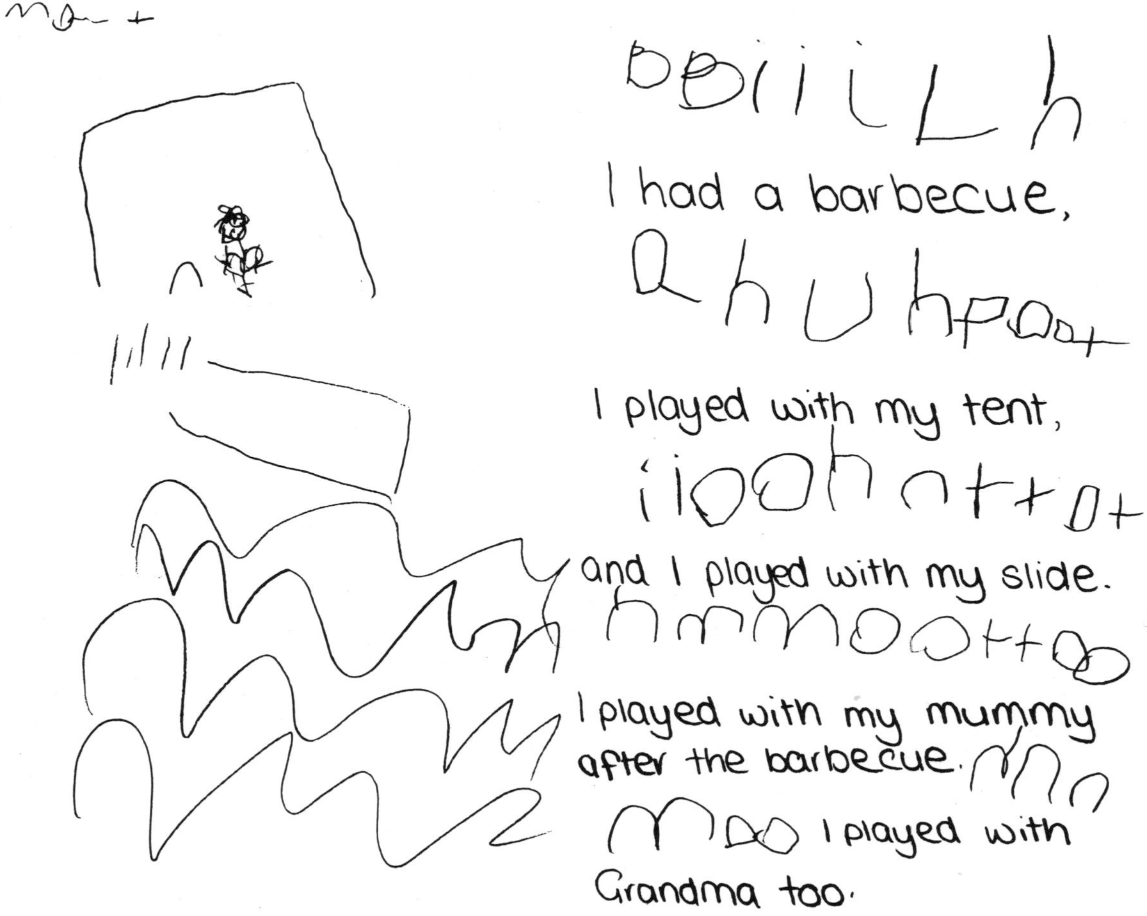

I had a barbecue,

I played with my tent,

and I played with my slide.

I played with my mummy after the barbecue. I played with Grandma too.

Figure 10.1 Max 'writing good'

together; she replied that she couldn't as her reading book was at school' (Miller, 1991, p. 3). After two terms in a reception class, Katie's view of reading was the book she either read in school or brought home from school. Like Katie, Lucy, studied by Baker and Raban (1991), started school knowing a lot about books and reading, although she was not reading in the conventional sense (Sulzby, 1990). Reading in Lucy's reception class involved reading books and a box of words to be learned at home. Continued observations of Lucy showed that she became less willing to work out for herself what a text might mean, she was reluctant to make the sort of 'good guesses' that she had in the past, which often were close approximations to the text. Baker and Raban express concern that over-emphasis on 'correct' performance by adults, shifts responsibility from young children from being 'active interpreters' of what they see, to depending upon the adult to provide solutions.

The role of the adult – parents

The role of the adult as a model for, and supporter and facilitator of, literacy development, occurs naturally for many children in the home setting, as described in Chapters 4 and 5. It was suggested that the adult's role in responding sensitively to the child's needs, knowing when to intervene, and when not to, knowing when to support and when to interact, is crucial in enabling the child to move forward in development. However, parents are uniquely placed to do this, as they have three key advantages over the professional educator:

- a unique knowledge of their child
- time for one-to-one interactions
- a natural context for literacy.

Early learning in the home setting is described by Munn and Schaffer (1993), as an 'ad hoc affair, with adults using opportunities to extend learning as they present themselves in the course of daily routines'. They go on to say, 'The very earliest learning which occurs in the home is relatively unplanned and is probably effective precisely because it is so informal' (p. 64). Parents who were invited to talk about the things they did to help to focus their children's attention on literacy and to support their learning described the following (Nutbrown, 1994, p. 89):

- Pointing out signs when on the bus and signs in shop windows.
- Looking at the labels on tins, naming the soup, spaghetti, other packages.
- Playing the part of a character in the book after reading it together.
- Looking at books, describing the pictures, saying which is a favourite and why.

- Putting up an alphabet poster on their bedroom wall, looking at letters and saying them.
- Making words from alphabet spaghetti at tea time.
- Choosing books together in the library.
- Reading adverts on TV and names that go up on the end of programmes such as *Neighbours.*
- Reading catalogues, helping to fill in the forms for the order.

A key difference between the role of parents and some professional educators is highlighted by Munn and Schaffer (1993), in effecting what they describe as children's entry to literacy, as 'mediating between children and artefacts rather than instructing them in the use of such artefacts' (p. 64).

The role of the adult – the professional educator

Because of their detailed and intimate knowledge of their child, parents are able to respond intuitively to their child's learning needs. Also, despite the hectic pace of life at home with young children, there is greater time available to spend in literacy events with an individual child, even if it is in the context of reading the label on the washing-up liquid as the dishes are washed or sharing a bedtime story. Opportunities for 'moment-to-moment' experiences with print (Taylor, 1986) are more likely to occur. Interacting in this way is a harder task for professional educators in pre-school centres, who are trying to meet the wide-ranging needs and demands of large groups of children. Therefore, in centre-based learning the adult will have a role which complements that of the parent or caregiver, however, it is not the same role, although some aspects will be shared.

The adult as model

Nutbrown (1994) and Campbell (1995) have suggested frameworks which describe ways in which the adult's role might be defined in encouraging emergent literacy development. These include to *model, provide, observe, interact, intervene, evaluate* (Nutbrown, 1994). In addition Campbell (1995) adds to *support, guide* and *instruct.* I would wish to add, the adult as *risk taker.*

The adult as risk taker

It takes courage to do things differently, to throw aside long-held assumptions about how adults teach and children learn. This is an understandable and shared concern. Harste *et al.* (1984, p. xix) confess:

> Teachers are often surprised to find, after becoming familiar with our current position, that as pre-school and elementary teachers we engaged in some of the practices we no longer condone. Our only justification is that at that time, such activities made sense. We now know more . . . and knowing more, we no longer engage children in such activities.

As they go on to say, 'Outgrowing one's current self is not easy.'

This moving on in a professional sense is eloquently described by Drummond (1993, p. 40):

> If I did not see, then, all that I wish I could see now, as I look back over these children's stories, it was not because there was less to see. It was because I had not then learned enough about the learning I was looking for; I had not yet understood how my own learning as a teacher could be fed and exercised by the close study of children's learning.

Some of the teachers and teachers in training with whom I work, express anxieties about allowing children opportunities to read and write within an emergent literacy framework. Others are, of course, already engaged in doing this. These anxieties are understandable, particularly for those professional educators working within the framework of the National Curriculum. Parents may also become anxious if they do not understand about emergent literacy and the adult's role in this, and this anxiety is transmitted to the professional educator.

A misconception about emergent literacy development is that the adult does not have a role, that children are left to learn 'naturally'. Hopefully this book has demonstrated that this is not the case. Adults, whether parents or professional educators, use a range of strategies in helping to move children on in their literacy development. Strategies used by teachers in moving children on towards conventional reading are described by Campbell (1992). 'Thus "natural" learning is in reality shaped and supported by adult intervention based on the child's needs and current level of ability' (Mandel-Morrow and Rand, 1991, p. 147).

As a member of the Manchester section of the National Writing Project, Price (1989), on being invited to a school to talk with the teachers about letter writing with young children, found that the nursery class had not been included; despite the fact that the nursery unit provided plenty of opportunities for the children to write. The nursery teacher said, 'Oh but the children in the nursery can't write letters so we didn't include them' (p. 1). This teacher's assumptions, like Alison's teacher, had prevented the children from demonstrating to her what they did know about letter writing.

Price's conviction that she could provide experiences which would 'illuminate for them some of the features involved in becoming an author of letters' (p. 1), led to a project based around Eric Carle's (1977) book,

The Bad Tempered Ladybird. The children had constructed a large model of a ladybird and seemed prepared to collude with the idea that it could be real, i.e. they talked about it and to it, and made things for it. Some time later they 'found' a letter in the classroom from the ladybird. This resulted in an exchange of letters in which the children revealed their varying knowledge of the writing system and which gave them insights into this particular form of writing.

Inspired by this account, one of my students initiated a similar project whilst carrying out a teaching experience in a school which had not previously encouraged emergent writing. Supported by the staff in her venture, she introduced the idea of a giant to a somewhat sceptical group of slightly older children. The arrival of an enormous letter, brought into the classroom a few days later by the school secretary, soon dispelled their disdain and fired them to begin a successful correspondence with the giant, using their emergent writing skills. As a result of the student's work in the school, the staff re-wrote their school policy on writing to include emergent writing. Thus, all of these adults were prepared to take risks in their professional practice, resulting in gains for themselves and the children.

The adult as model

Children need to see adults modelling literacy in all the settings described in the previous chapter, in cafes, shops, offices, the book area and in the context of their own role; for example reading books and print around the room, writing messages or letters for parents, writing notices and labels for displays. As Campbell (1994) says, 'Imagine how difficult it must be to construct a concept of literacy if reading and writing are never witnessed' (p. 3). In doing this adults will be demonstrating what print is, how it is used and in which contexts (Nutbrown, 1994).

The adult as provider

If settings such as those described in the previous chapter are provided, the adult will have gone some considerable way towards supporting the literacy development of the children in their care. Children will have been provided with the equipment and materials required to engage in literacy-related activities. These will relate to models of literacy which are familiar to the children (Gregory and Rashid, 1992–3; Gregory and Biarnès, 1994; Nutbrown, 1994).

The adult as observer

The role of the adult in observing young children from an informed perspective was stressed in Chapter 8. In order to know when and how to support, intervene or interact, adults need to observe what young children do and say in literacy contexts (Nutbrown, 1994). It is through informed observation that assessment occurs; it is how we find out what children know about reading and writing. However, assessment is not the final stage of the process; the adult will also have a role in evaluating what was observed, that is, reflecting upon and reviewing what happened (Drummond, 1993; Nutbrown, 1994). This can be framed as:

- What did the child already know about literacy?
- What did the child learn about literacy?
- Was the adult's intervention, interaction, support, guidance or exchange a successful strategy?
- What will the adult do next to support the child's literacy development?

The adult as supporter

At the onset of this chapter it was stated that provision for literacy, although important, is not enough. As Munn and Schaffer (1994) note, 'the environment of even very young children is full of aspects relating to literacy'; pre-school centres are included in this. They suggest literacy materials 'are usually found in abundance in nurseries' (p. 75). However, what they go on to say is that the issue is not the availability of such items, but the adults' role in drawing children into meaningful use of the material.

A factor identified by Munn and Schaffer (1994) in enabling the professional educator to give sensitive support to young children in literacy contexts in pre-school centres was the way in which adults were organized in the nurseries they observed. Nurseries in which adults were able to form close relationships with 'their' group of children allowed for a role closer to that of the parent. This allows the professional educator to get to know the children and to provide literacy experiences appropriate to them. Thus the adult as *supporter* can *interact, intervene, guide, encourage* and *instruct,* in order to participate in meaningful literacy exchanges with the children in their care.

The observations carried out by Munn and Schaffer (1994) suggested that organizing children into small groups with a key adult resulted in enhanced literacy experiences for the children. Adults working in reception classes with poor adult–child staffing ratios may need to enlist extra adults, in addition to any paid support they may have. In a report on 4-year-olds in infant classes, Cleave and Brown (1991) have said, 'Children of this age need a sufficient number of adults to help them to feel secure and confident' (p. 186). They noted that parents seemed to be the key source of help, but also that volunteers and young people engaged in training schemes were encouraged to be involved.

This chapter has argued that sensitive and responsive adults, who are in tune with each child's needs, are crucial in supporting and facilitating children's literacy development in the home and in pre-school centres. It has been suggested that learning about literacy in these two settings is complimentary, but different. The role of parents' and professional educators have many shared aspects, but are, nevertheless, not the same; learning about literacy in the home being relatively unplanned. What is important, is that both parents and professional educators work together in the pre-school years, in order to provide for continuity of learning between home and pre-school.

CHAPTER 11

Continuity between home and pre-school

In considering the role of the professional educator in encouraging and supporting children's literacy development, it has been suggested that adults work within particular frameworks, which in turn affect their practice. This framework will determine what might be described as the 'culture' of a particular setting. The framework within which this book has been written is that of an 'emergent literacy' perspective. This particular way of viewing how I believe many young children come to know about literacy in the early years, has been affected by my own involvement as a parent and professional educator, and by the writing and experience of others. I believe that as professional educators we need to offer children literacy experiences, particularly in the pre-school years, which to some extent replicate and certainly build upon their encounters with literacy in the home (Miller, 1991). It is important to note, however, that for some children, the culture of the pre-school setting, including the ways in which literacy is experienced and presented, will be very different and 'distanced' from the setting of the home.

Gregory and Biarnès (1994) describe how Tony, a Chinese child whose family moved to England from Hong Kong, 'switched off' from books in his multi-lingual reception class, despite the efforts of the teacher and school to ensure the school setting reflected the community it served. A visit by the teacher to Tony's home revealed the extent of the distance between home and school. Tony's family considered that books should only be given when they have been 'earned'. They believed that his books from school should be kept until he was able to read the words. Similarly, Tony's attempts at writing 'ToNy' were described by his grandfather as 'rubbish', as he showed the teacher the immaculate ideographs Tony had filled his book with at his Chinese Saturday school. It is evident that Tony's family and teacher have very different views of what constitutes school and learning. This poses a dilemma for the professional educator. Flooding the classroom with bi-lingual books and print featuring languages other than English, will not provide an answer. One answer may be for the professional educator to explain more clearly to parents what they do, and why they do it in this way.

Gregory and Biarnès (1994) argue that to some extent the school (and I would include the pre-school) setting is a 'new world' for all children in terms of language and behaviour. They suggest that a role for the professional educator may be that of a 'mediator' who facilitates each child's entry into this new world. For a child such as Tony, this may involve valuing and displaying within the classroom his considerable skills learned in Chinese school. It will also involve the professional educator in finding ways to involve and support Tony and his family, in ways which reduce the distance between home and school. For other children, who have had little experience of books and print, they will require literacy experiences not yet encountered (Miller, 1991; OFSTED, 1993). For still others, literacy in pre-school centres will be part of the continuum of emerging literacy, whose roots will have been firmly established in the home.

References

Adams, M.J. (1990) *Beginning to Read: Thinking and Learning about Print.* Cambridge, Mass.: MIT Press.

Ahlberg, A. and Ahlberg, J. (1977) *Burglar Bill.* London: Heinemann.

Ahlberg, J. and Ahlberg, A. (1986) *The Jolly Postman or Other People's Letters.* London: Heinemann.

Anbar, A. (1986) Reading acquisition of pre-school children without systematic instruction, *Early Childhood Research Quarterly*, 1: 69–83.

Andreae, J., Burke, J., Bushell, R., Chandri, J., Healey, M., Lindley, M., Norman, K., Schaffer, J., Stockdale, M., Veitch, B. and Wilson, A. (1988) *Early Literacy Project.* Manchester City Council Education Department.

Baker, P. and Raban, B. (1991) Reading before and after the early days of schooling, *Reading*, 25 (1): 6–12.

Ball, C. (1994) *Start Right.* London: RSA.

Barrs, M., Ellis, S., Hester, M. and Thomas, A. (1988) *The Primary Language Record.* London: Centre for Language in Primary Education.

Bartholomew, L. and Bruce, T. (1993) *Getting to Know You: A Guide to Record Keeping in Early Childhood Education and Care.* London: Hodder and Stoughton.

Beard, R. (1987) Battle of the books, *Child Education*, 12–13.

Bennet, J. (1985) *Learning to Read with Picture Books.* Stroud: Thimble Press.

Bissex, G.L. (1980) *Gnys at Wrk: A Child Learns to Write and Read.* London: Harvard University Press.

Blackstone, T. (1971) *A Fair Start.* London: Penguin.

Bloom, W. (1987) *Partnership with Parents in Reading.* London: Hodder and Stoughton with UKRA.

Bronfenbrenner, U. (1975) Is early intervention effective? In Friedlander, B.S. (eds) *Exceptional Infants: Assessment and Intervention.* New York: Bruner/Mazel.

Bruce, T. (1991) *Time to Play in Early Childhood.* London: Hodder and Stoughton.

Bruner, J. (1975) The ontogenesis of speech acts, *Journal of Child Language*, 2: 1–19.

Bruner, J.S. (1977) Early social interaction and language acquisition. In Schaffer, H.R. (ed.) *Studies in Mother Infant Interaction.* London: Academic Press.

Bryant, P. and Bradley, L. (1985) *Children's Reading Problems.* Oxford: Basil Blackwell.

Campbell, R. (1992) *Reading Real Books.* Milton Keynes: Open University Press.

Campbell, R. (1994) Modelling literacy in the nursery classroom, *Early Education*, 12: 3–4.

Campbell, R. (1995) The role of the adult in supporting literacy development. In Campbell, R. and Miller, L. (eds) *Supporting Children in the Early Years.* Stoke-on-Trent: Trentham Books.

Carle, E. (1970) *The Very Hungry Caterpillar.* London: Hamish Hamilton.

Carle, E. (1977) *The Bad Tempered Ladybird.* Middlesex: Puffin Books.

Chukovsky, K. (1971) *From Two to Five.* Berkeley: University of California Press.

Clark, M.M. (1976) *Young Fluent Readers.* London: Heinemann Educational.

Clay, M. (1975) *What Did I Write?* London: Heinemann Educational.

Clay, M. (1977) *Reading: The Patterning of Complex Behaviour.* London: Heinemann Educational.

Clay, M. (1979) *STONES – the Concepts about Print Test.* Auckland, New Zealand: Heinemann Educational.

Clay, M.M. (1989) Concepts about print in English and other languages, *The Reading Teacher*, 42 (4): 268–76.

Cleave, S. and Brown, S. (1991) *Early to School: Four Year Olds in Infant Classes.* Windsor: NFER/Nelson.

Cooper, J. (1987) Book share: involving parents in nursery literacy, *Reading*, 21 (2): 99–106.

Cornell, E.H., Senechal, M. and Broda, L.S. (1988) Recall of picture books by 3 year old children: testing and repetition effects in joint reading activities, *Journal of Educational Psychology*, 80 (4): 537–42.

Croall, J. (1993) A family of skills, *Co-ordinate*, 36: 4–5.

Currie, L.A. and Bowes, A. (1988) A head start to learning: involving parents of children just about to start school, *Support for Learning*, 3 (4): 196–200.

Davies, A. (1988) Children's names: bridges to literacy, *Research in Education*, 40: 19–31.

DES (1990) *Starting with Quality.* London: HMSO.

Donaldson, M. (1978) *Children's Minds.* Glasgow: Fontana/Collins.

Donaldson, M. (1984) Speech and writing and modes of learning. In Goelman, H., Oberg, A. and Smith, F. (eds) *Awakening to Literacy.* London: Heinemann Educational.

Downing, J. and Thackray, D.V. (1972) An appraisal of reading readiness. In Melnik, A. and Merritt, J. (eds) *The Reading Curriculum.* London: University of London Press/Open University Press.

Drummond, M.J. (1993) *Assessing Children's Learning.* London: David Fulton.

Drummond, M.J. and Nutbrown, C. (1992) Observing and assessing young children. In Pugh, G. (ed.) *Contemporary Issues in the Early Years: Working Collaboratively for Young Children.* London: Paul Chapman/National Children's Bureau.

Early Years Curriculum Group (1989) *Early Childhood Education: The Early Years Curriculum and the National Curriculum.* Stoke-on-Trent: Trentham Books.

Early Years Curriculum Group (1992) *First Things First: Educating Young Children.* Oldham: Madeleine Lindley Ltd.

Ferreiro, E. (1984) The underlying logic of literacy development. In Goelman, H., Oberg, A. and Smith, F. (eds) *Awakening to Literacy.* London: Heinemann Educational.

Fox, C. (1992) 'You sing so merry those tunes': oral storytelling as a window on young children's language learning. In Kimberley, K., Meek, M. and Miller, J. (eds) *New Readings: Contributions to an Understanding of Literacy.* London: A & C Black.

Fox, C. (1994) Oral storytelling with young children. Paper delivered at early years seminars: supporting children in the early years: from research to practice. University of Hertfordshire. 19 April.

Gaines, K. (1988) The nursery library projects: reading as a recreational activity. Unpublished paper presented to the UKRA Conference, Edinburgh.

Geekie, P. and Raban, B. (1993) *Learning to Read and Write Through Classroom Talk.* Stoke-on-Trent: Trentham Books.

Gentry, J.R. (1982) An analysis of developmental spelling in Gnys at Work, *The Reading Teacher,* 36 (2): 193–9.

Goodall, M. (1984) Can four year olds 'read' words in the environment?, *The Reading Teacher,* 37: 478–82.

Goodman, Y.M. (1982) Concepts about print. In Clay, M.M. (ed.) *Observing Young Readers: Selected Papers.* London: Heinemann Educational.

Goodman, Y. (1984) The development of initial literacy. In Goelman, H., Oberg, A. and Smith, F. (eds) *Awakening to Literacy.* London: Heinemann Educational.

Goswami, U. (1994) Phonological skills, analogies and reading development, *Reading,* 28 (2): 32–7.

Goswami, U. and Bryant, P. (1990) *Phonological Skills and Learning to Read.* Hove: Laurence Erlbaum Associates.

Gregory, E. (1992) Learning codes and contexts: a psychosemiotic approach to beginning reading in school. In Kimberley, K., Meek, M. and Miller, J. (eds) *New Readings: Contributions to an Understanding of Literacy.* London: A & C Black.

Gregory, E. and Biarnès, J. (1994) Tony and Jean Franois looking for sense in the strangeness of school. In Dombey, H. and Meek-Spencer, M. (eds) *First Steps Together: Home School Early Literacy in European Contexts.* Stoke-on-Trent: Trentham Books/IEDPE.

Gregory, E. and Rashid, N. (1992–3) The Tower Hamlets work: monolingual schooling, multilingual homes. In Gregory, E., Lathwell, J., Mace, J. and Rashid, N. (eds) *Literacy at Home and at School.* London: Goldsmiths College Faculty of Education.

Griffiths, A. and Edmonds, M. (1988) *Report on The Calderdale Pre-School Project.* Calderdale: School Psychological Service, Borough of Calderdale Education Department.

Hall, N. (1985) When do children learn to read?, *Reading,* 19 (2): 57–69.

Hall, N. (1987) *The Emergence of Literacy.* London: Edward Arnold.

Hall, N. (1988) Nursery children's views about reading and writing. In Anderson, C. (ed.) *Reading: The abc and Beyond.* Basingstoke: Macmillan.

Hall, N. (1991) Play and the emergence of literacy. In Christie, J.F. (ed.) *Play and Early Literacy Development.* Albany: State University of New York Press.

Hannon, P. and James, S. (1990) Parents' and teachers' perspectives on pre-school literacy development, *British Educational Research Journal,* 16 (3): 259–72.

Hannon, P. and Weinberger, J. (1994) Sharing new ideas about literacy with parents. In Dombey, H. and Meek-Spencer, M. (eds) *First Steps Together: Home School Literacy in European Contexts.* Stoke-on-Trent: Trentham Books/IEDPE.

Harman, H. (1993) *The Century Gap.* London: Ebury Press.

Harrison, M.L. and Stroud, J.B. (1956) *The Harrison–Stroud Reading Readiness Profiles.* Boston: Houghton Mifflin Company.

Harste, J.C., Woodward, V.A. and Burke, C.L. (1984) *Language Stories and Literacy Lessons.* Portsmouth, New Hampshire: Heinemann Educational.

Hartley, D. and Quine, P. (1982) A critical appraisal of Marie Clay's 'Concepts about Print' test, *Reading,* 16 (2): 109–12.

Heath, S.B. (1982) What no bedtime story means: narrative skills at home and at school, *Language in Society,* 11: 49–75.

Hertfordshire County Council (1993) *Early Years Record of Achievement.* The Education Centre, Butterfield Road, Wheathampstead, AL4 8PY.

Hiebert, E.H. (1978) Pre-school children's understanding of written language, *Child Development,* 49: 1231–4.

HMI (1989) *Aspects of Primary Education: The Education of Children under Five.* London: HMSO.

HMI (1990) *The Teaching and Learning of Reading in Primary Schools.* London: HMSO.

Holdaway, D. (1979) *The Foundation of Literacy.* London: Ashton Scholastic.

Hopkins, D.A. (1985) *A Teachers Guide to Classroom Research.* Milton Keynes: Open University Press.

Hurst, V. (1994) Searching for quality. Paper delivered at BAECE Conference, 'Why Nursery Education?'. Church House Conference Centre, Westminster, 29 September.

James, H. and Wyeth, M. (1994) The Primary Language Record: parents and teachers learning together. In Dombey, H. and Meek-Spencer, M. (eds) *First Steps Together: Home Early School Literacy in European Contexts.* Stoke-on-Trent: Trentham/IEDPE.

Jordan, R. and Powell, S. (1990) High/Scope – a cautionary view, *Early Years,* 11 (1): 29–38.

Kontos, S. (1986) What pre school children know about reading and how they learn it, *Young Children,* November: 58–66.

Kumar, V. (1993) *Poverty and Inequality in the U.K.: The Effects on Children.* London: National Children's Bureau.

Lally, M. (1991) *The Nursery Teacher in Action.* London: Paul Chapman Publishing.

Laminack, L.L. (1991) *Learning with Zachary.* Richmond Hill, Ontario: Ashton Scholastic.

Langdown, A. (1989) *Getting Started: A Teacher's Experience of High/Scope.* London: VOLCUF.

Lass, B. (1983) Portrait of my son as an early reader II, *The Reading Teacher,* 36 (6): 508–15.

Leichter, H.J. (1984) Families as environments for literacy. In Goelman, H., Oberg, A. and Smith, F. (eds) *Awaking to Literacy.* London: Heinemann Educational.

Lomax, R.G. and McGee, L.M. (1987) Young children's concepts about print and reading: towards a model of word reading acquisition, *Reading Research Quarterly,* XXII (2): 237–52.

Madeleine Lindley Ltd. Book Centre, 79 and 90 Acorn Centre, Barry Street, Oldham, OL1 3NE.

Manchester City Council Education Department (1993a) *Assessment and Record Keeping in the Early Years.* Manchester: IAS Publications.

Manchester City Council Education Department (1993b) *English in the National Curriculum: Key Stage One Resource Pack.* Manchester: IAS Publications.

Mandel-Morrow, L. (1988) Young children's responses to one to one story readings in school settings, *Reading Research Quarterly*, 23 (1): 89–107.

Mandel-Morrow, L. and Rand, M. (1991) Preparing the classroom environment to promote literacy during play. In Christie, J.F. (ed.) *Play and Early Literacy Development.* Albany, New York: State University of New York Press.

Mason, J. (1980) When do children begin to read?: an exploration of four year old children's letter and word reading competences, *Reading Research Quarterly*, 15 (2): 203–27.

Masonheimer, P.E., Drum, P.A. and Ellis, L.C. (1984) Does environmental print identification lead children into word reading?, *Journal of Reading Behaviour*, 16: 257–71.

Meek, M. (1982) *Learning to Read.* London: Bodley Head.

Meek, M. (1988) *How Texts Teach What Readers Learn.* Stroud: Thimble Press.

Meek, M. (1991) *Learning to be Literate.* London: Bodley Head.

Meek, M. (1993) Reading in the balance, *Child Education*, October: 31–55.

Miller, L. (1990) Sharing books in the pre-school: what's it all about?, *Early Years*, 11 (1): 13–17.

Miller, L. (1991) Literacy development in young children: continuity between home and school, *Early Education*, 4: 3–5.

Miller, L. (1992) 'A share-a-book scheme in a pre-school playgroup', unpublished M Phil thesis. University of Hertfordshire.

Mittler, P. and Mittler, H. (1982) *Partnership with Parents.* Stratford-upon-Avon: National Council for Special Education.

Munn, P. and Schaffer, R.H. (1993) Evenements relatits a la capacite de lecture, d'ecriture et de calcul dans des contextes interactifs socioux, *International Journal of Early Years Education*, 1 (3): 61–80.

Neuman, S.B. and Roskos, K. (1991) The influence of literacy – enriched play centers on pre-schoolers conceptions of the functions of print. In Christie, J.F. (ed.) *Play and Early Literacy Development.* Albany: State University of New York Press.

Nutbrown, C. (1994) *Threads of Thinking: Young Children Learning and the Role of Education.* London: Paul Chapman Publishing.

Nutbrown, C. and Hannon, P. (1993) Assessing early literacy – new methods needed, *International Journal of Early Childhood*, 25 (2): 27–30.

OFSTED (1993) *The Teaching and Learning of Reading and Writing in Reception Classes and Year 1.* London: Office for Standards in Education Publications Centre.

Parlett, M. and Hamilton, D. (1977) Evaluation as illumination: a new approach to the study of innovatory programmes. In Jenkins, D., King, C., MacDonald, B., Parlett, M. and Hamilton, D. (eds) *Beyond the Numbers Game.* London: Macmillan Education.

Pascal, C. (1990) *Under Fives in Infant Classrooms.* Stoke-on-Trent: Trentham Books.

Payton, S. (1984) *Developing Awareness of Print: A Young Child's First Steps Towards Literacy.* University of Birmingham: Educational Review, Offset Publication, No. 2.

Pearson, H. (1990) Stories and learning to read, *Reading*, 24 (2): 57–65.

Phillips, G. and McNaughton, S. (1990) The practice of storybook reading to pre-school children in mainstream New Zealand families, *Reading Research Quarterly*, XXV (3): 196–211.

Price, J. (1989) The ladybird letters. In Hall, N. (ed.) *Writing with Reason*. London: Hodder and Stoughton.

Robson, C. and Whitley, S. (1989) Sharing stories: parents' involvement in reading with inner city nursery children, *Reading*, 23 (1): 23–7.

Sheridan, M.D. (1975) *Children's Developmental Progress*. Windsor: NFER.

Smith, A. (1993) Early childhood educare: seeking a theoretical framework in Vygotsky's work, *International Journal of Early Years Education*, 1 (1): 47–60.

Smith, F. (1984) The creative achievement of literacy. In Goelman, H., Oberg, A. and Smith, F. (eds) *Awakening to Literacy*. London, New Hampshire: Heinemann Educational.

Smith, F. (1985) *Reading* (2nd edn). Cambridge: Cambridge University Press.

Smith, F. (1986) *Misleading Metaphors of Literacy*. Victoria, BC: Abel Press, Reading and Language Information Centre.

Smith, W. (1987) *The Witch Baby*. Middlesex: Picture Puffins.

Snow, C. and Nino, A. (1986) The contracts of literacy: what children learn from learning to read books. In Teale, W. and Sulzby, E. (eds) in *Emergent Literacy: Writing and Reading*. New Jersey: Ablex Publishing Corporation.

Snow, C., Nathan, D. and Perlmann, R. (1985) Assessing children's knowledge about book reading. In Galda, L. and Pellegrini, A.D. (eds) *The Development of Children's Literate Behaviour*. New York: Ablex Publishing Corporation.

Spencer, D. (1994) Tool kit to fix family literacy, *Times Educational Supplement*, 3 June.

Story Chest (1982, ongoing series). Surrey: Thomas Nelson and Sons.

Strongin Dodds, L. (1994) Learning together: programmes for parents, *Co-ordinate*, 39: 12–13.

Sulzby, E. (1986) Writing and reading: signs of oral and written language organisation in the young child. In Teale, W.H. and Sulzby, E. (eds) *Emergent Literacy*. New Jersey: Ablex Publishing Corporation.

Sulzby, E. (1990) Assessment of writing and children's language while writing. In Mandel-Morrow, L. and Smith, J.K. (eds) *Assessment for Instruction in Early Literacy*. New Jersey: Prentice-Hall.

Sulzby, E., Teale, W.H. and Kamberelis, G. (1989) Emergent writing in the classroom: home and school connections. In Strickland, D.S. and Mandel-Morrow, L. (eds) *Emerging Literacy: Young Children Learn to Read and Write*. Newark, Delaware: International Reading Association.

Taylor, D. (1982) Translating children's everyday use of print into classroom practice, *Language Arts*, 59 (6): 547–9.

Taylor, D. (1983) *Family Literacy: Young Children Learn to Read and Write*. Exeter, New Hampshire: Heinemann Educational.

Taylor, D. (1986) Creating family story: 'Mathew! We're going to have a ride'. In Teale, W. and Sulzby, E. (eds) *Emergent Literacy: Writing and Reading*. New Jersey: Ablex Publishing Corporation.

Taylor, D. and Strickland, S. (1986) *Family Storybook Reading*. Portsmouth, New Hampshire: Heinemann Educational.

Taylor, D. and Walls, L. (1990) Educating parents about their children's early literacy development, *The Reading Teacher*, 44 (1): 72–4.

Teale, W.H. (1981) Parents reading to their children: what we know and need to know, *Language Arts*, 58: 902–11.

Teale, W.H. (1984) Reading to young children: it's significance for literacy development. In Goelman, H., Oberg, A. and Smith, F. (eds) *Awakening to Literacy*. London: Heinemann Educational.

Teale, W. (1986) Home background and young children's literacy development. In Teale, W. and Sulzby, E. (eds) *Emergent Literacy: Writing and Reading*. New Jersey: Ablex Publishing Corporation.

Teale, W.H. (1990) The promise and challenge of informal assessment in early literacy, in Morrow, L.M. and Smith, J.K. (eds) *Assessment for Instruction in Early Literacy*. New Jersey: Prentice-Hall.

Teale, W.H. and Sulzby, E. (1986) Emergent literacy as a perspective for examining how young children become writers and readers. In Teale, W.H. and Sulzby, E. (eds) *Emergent Literacy: Writing and Reading*. New Jersey: Ablex Publishing Corporation.

Tizard, B. and Hughes, M. (1984) *Young Children Learning: Talking and Thinking at Home and at School*. London: Fontana.

Tizard, B., Blatchford, P., Burke, J., Farquhars, C. and Plewis, C. (1988) *Young Children at School in the Inner City*. Hove: Laurence Erlbaum Associates.

Topping, K. (1985) Parental involvement in reading: theoretical and empirical background. In Topping, K. and Wolfendale, S. (eds) *Parental Involvement in Children's Reading*. London: Croom Helm.

Vygotsky, L.S. (1978) *Mind in Society: the Development of Higher Mental Processes*. Cambridge, Mass.: Harvard University Press.

Waterland, L. (1985) *Read With Me*. Stroud: Thimble Press.

Weinberger, J. (1988) Reading, parents and pre-school. *Reading*, 22 (3): 164–7.

Weinberger, J., Hannon, P. and Nutbrown, C. (1990) *Ways of Working with Parents to Promote Literacy Development*. Sheffield: University of Sheffield, Division of Education.

Wells, G. (1985) *Language Learning and Education*. Windsor: NFER/Nelson.

Wells, G. (1987) *The Meaning Makers: Children Learning Language and Using Language to Learn*. London: Heinemann Educational.

Whitehead, F., Capey, A.C., Maddren, W. and Wellings, A. (1975) *Children and their Books*. Basingstoke: Macmillan Education.

Wolf, S.A. and Heath, S.B. (1992) *The Braid of Literature*. London: Harvard University Press.

Wolfendale, S. (1985) Overview of parental participation in childrens education. In Topping, K. and Wolfendale, S. (eds) *Parental Involvement in Children's Reading*. London: Croom Helm.

Yaden, D.B. Jr, Smolkin, L.B. and Conlon, A. (1989) Pre-schoolers' questions about pictures, print conventions and story text during reading aloud at home, *Reading Research Quarterly*, XXIV (2): 188–215.

Index